Dirty Laundry

*Why adults with ADHD are so ashamed
and what we can do to help*

Richard Pink & Roxanne Emery

TEN SPEED PRESS
California | New York

This book aims to provide useful information based on the authors' personal experience, but it is not intended to replace your doctor's medical advice.

Published in the United States by Ten Speed Press, an imprint of the Crown Publishing Group, a division of Penguin Random House LLC, New York.
TenSpeed.com
Crownpublishing.com

Ten Speed Press and the Ten Speed Press colophon are registered trademarks of Penguin Random House LLC.

Originally published in the United Kingdom by Square Peg, an imprint of Vintage, a division of Penguin Random House UK, in 2023.

Cover photograph courtesy of iStock
Cover design: x2design

Library of Congress Control Number: 2023939408

Trade Paperback ISBN: 978-0-593-83553-1
eBook ISBN: 978-0-593-83554-8

Printed in the United States of America

Acquiring editor: Molly Birnbaum | Project editor: Gabby Ureña Matos
Production manager: Dan Myers
Marketer: Brianne Sperber

10 9 8 7 6 5 4

First US Edition

Contents

@ADHD_LOVE: Our Origin Story

Hi—nice to meet you. I'm Rich. My wife Rox and I run the social media accounts ADHD_Love. Over the last year our videos have been viewed more than 200 million times, and we've built a community of people looking to learn about *real* life with ADHD. If you don't mind, I'd love to tell you a little bit about how all of this started...

One evening, I rolled over to my partner and asked if she had a tampon in. This may seem like a rather strange question to ask your wife. *Is this dude for real?!* I hear you thinking. *That's really weird, and a bit controlling—major red flag.* No pun intended.

Normally, I'd agree with you. However, when you are married to someone with ADHD, this is just the kind of question you find yourself asking.

You see, my wife forgets that she has periods. Despite the monthly reminders, for almost two decades, every new period is kind of like a first for her. "Oh, wow," she'll say to me. "I'm on my period, babe." And then she'll look at me, shocked, as though she can't believe it.

A couple of years before this, we were halfway round the hardest route at a place called Go Ape, an outdoor assault course built into the trees, when she made her monthly discovery. You can't climb down, and you certainly can't nip to Boots; all you can do is make the best of the situation at hand. In this case, my wife noticing she's on her period.

I check my pockets, and, thank God, I have a packet of tissues. "Will these work?" I ask, handing them to her.

"Absolutely," she says confidently. "I'll just make a trampon."

A trampon is not something I had heard of prior to meeting my wife. It doesn't appear in the Oxford Dictionary, so you'll just have to trust me with this one...

Trampon: *noun*; a self-rolled tampon, often made of toilet roll, and employed by neurodivergents who may have left the house without sanitary products.

My ADHD wife has been rolling trampons since secondary school. So, 30 metres in the air, at a Kentish countryside Go Ape, I watched her execute what can only be described as an extraordinary accomplishment of skill and bravery—yet, one I couldn't help feel was slightly unnecessary.

Since that occasion, I have taken it upon myself to check in with my wife every month, alerting her it's almost period time, rather like a friendly, bearded tracking app, and ensuring that she is wearing Tampax-certified sanitary products, rather than the DIY versions.

So, back to the night in question at the beginning of this story. After I asked my wife if she had a tampon in, she rolled over and sleepily replied, "Yes." You'll understand now why I couldn't just leave my enquiry there.

"Can I just check it's not a trampon, that it's a real tampon?"

"Real tampon," she replied, a proud little smile spreading across her face.

That sorted, we were both peacefully drifting off to sleep when she suddenly yelled "BABE!" and sat bolt upright in bed. "That whole interaction would make an amazing TikTok."

It was 11.55 p.m. But even half asleep, I could see how that moment would be a pretty hilarious thing to share on social media. "Great idea, babe," I said. "Let's get some sleep and we can start the account tomorrow."

As the words left my mouth, though, I knew I was fighting a losing battle. You see, my wife had *the glint* in her eye. A glint that has had me redecorating the living room at two a.m., ordering a pizza when we're meant to be dieting, and buying all the equipment required to start a resin business. The glint means, "Not a chance am I going to sleep. This needs to happen *now*."

I've learned to fight certain aspects of my wife's ADHD. For instance, I refuse to have a "floordrobe" (an untidy heap of discarded clothing) in our bedroom; I encourage her to shower more than once a week; and I am in charge of all our credit cards due to bankruptcy-worthy levels of debt she managed to run up in years gone by. But the glint? Not a chance. In this moment, she is Muhammad Ali. Unstoppable. Unbeatable.

I sat up in bed, resigned to my defeat.

Fifteen minutes of ADHD super-speed brainstorming later, our ADHD_Love TikTok account was created, and our first video, "REAL TAMPON," was live. Exhausted, we both snuggled down to sleep... with no idea that we had just done something that would alter the course of the rest of our lives. That this video about my wife's self-rolled tampons would go viral, that we would continue to create ADHD content and build a community of millions.

And that, ultimately, this would be the decision that would lead to you holding this book in your hands right now.

So here's to ADHD. And here's to the glint in my wife's eye.

INTRODUCTION: WHY IS EVERYONE CRYING?!

One of the weirdest things that has happened to us both over the last year, is that people who have seen our social media accounts have begun stopping us in the street. It's always such a wonderful reminder of the real humans who are watching what we create. Something that has shocked me, though, is that the majority of people we've met have started crying.

The reason I find that odd is that our account is what I think most people would call a comedy account. It's meant to be humorous. I'm not saying either of us is the next Ricky Gervais (although if you saw the pyjama-clad dance moves she pulls before bed, you might start to believe it), but on the whole we create light-hearted moments from our life and share them on the internet. So why were people crying?

After this had happened a few times, I turned to my wife as we were walking away from a young woman who had stopped us in Canterbury. Baffled, I whispered, "Babe... why was she crying? Did I say something wrong?"

One thing I've learned is that neurodivergent people are incredibly sensitive. I don't mean that in the way society does, as some kind of negative, some kind of too-much-ness—I mean it in the best way. The neurodivergent people I know are really connected to themselves and those around them, so when one of them starts crying, I genuinely wonder where I've gone wrong.

Of course, my ADHD wife knew exactly why this young woman, and all the rest of the people we met, were crying. It's almost like they speak the same language, an unwritten dialogue of understanding that comes, ironically, from a lifetime of being misunderstood. She knew why they were crying because she's one of them.

And now, at this point, I'd like to introduce you to my ADHD wife, Rox.

MEET MY ADHD WIFE

Hi, I'm Rox, AKA *the ADHD wife!* I'm so happy that I get to talk to you. First, let me remind you to go take the washing out of the dryer, and second, I'll pick up where Rich left off and explain why people we meet start crying.

It's shame. The same shame I had felt for my entire life, until I received an ADHD diagnosis at age 36 and, soon afterward, became part of an incredible internet community of people just like me. I remember my first time watching an "ADHD Symptoms" video on TikTok, before I knew I had it. I burst into tears. For the first time in my life, my inner monologue, my strange and very weird struggles, were being shared by somebody else. I remember being struck so clearly by the following words: *Oh my god, it isn't just me.*

Growing up with undiagnosed ADHD left me feeling utterly broken for many years. I was constantly torn between my desperate need to achieve my "gifted child" potential and my personal shame over the fact I couldn't make my bed, do my washing, or take care of my finances. When you stack years of feeling like a failure on top of each other, you get a person with rock-bottom self-esteem. There's a sense of despair at the fact that you just cannot get hold of your life no matter how hard you try. You feel judged by your family; you're the black sheep, the failure, the one who always quits, the one who's always late, the one who will never make it… You become somebody who is ashamed of themselves. Can you guess how people who are ashamed of themselves live? I'll give you a hint: dangerously. Drink, drugs, sex, shopping. Anything to avoid the pain of being themselves. Needless to say, the pursuit of those things, although it brings temporary relief, only leads you to an even darker place.

I get to share the light-hearted moments now, only because I somehow made it through the really dark ones. These are moments that won't ever be shared on the internet because I was genuinely struggling to stay alive. I remember being sat in a pitch-black apartment, after my electricity was cut off for late payment, surrounded by empty bottles that had contained the alcohol I used to self-medicate the anxiety, wishing the pain would stop.

Getting to create content now, and reach people who may be struggling like I once did, is an absolute privilege. I am so lucky to have had therapy, to be sober, and to have met the most incredible partner. However, to get back to Rich's point, I'm not surprised that when we meet people like me, they very often begin to cry. I know the dark nights that people with an ADHD diagnosis have had to get through, often alone. I know the shame that living undiagnosed can bring, and I know the absolute relief of watching a 30-second video on TikTok and being able to breathe for the first time in 30 years, because *Oh my god, it isn't just me.*

HOW TO READ THIS BOOK

This book explores a collection of ten symptoms. You know, the top ten you've read when you've Googled "symptoms of ADHD"— forgetfulness, impulsivity, difficulties with money, and so on.

Reading the symptoms, whether it's on the NHS website or on an internet meme, does not give the full picture of the struggles of life with ADHD. One-word lists of symptoms are incredibly vague; they also allow for the common trope of "Oh well, everybody's a bit like that." Yes, everybody can be a bit forgetful. But has everybody lost eight sets of iPhone headphones in the LAST SIX MONTHS?

We want to put real, messy, personal stories to the symptoms: no holds barred, no trampon unturned. You'll learn about some of my greatest challenges, and how I've found a way to not only manage my ADHD, but to work with my partner to create a warm, safe, compassionate and often hilarious home life. Which is what we want for you too.

A little disclaimer moment here: of course, all ADHDers are different. My symptoms may be different to yours. I don't mean to invalidate you by sharing mine. We're sharing our stories with you in the hope of reducing some of the shame that comes with living with ADHD, to give ADHDers and their partners a road map for a happier and more connected life.

For each symptom, you'll hear an anecdote from me, many from the darker days of my undiagnosed life, as well as how Rich and I deal with these symptoms currently. Over and over again, we will return to our two essential tools: non-judgement and compassion.

The power of these tools is undeniable. For example, I have beaten myself up my whole life for not being able to make my bed. I've called myself awful names because of it: *Stupid, useless, an absolute loser, an utter disgrace.* I've also been heavily judged by others. "Come on now… making a bed is not difficult. Stop seeking attention and just admit you are being lazy." Newsflash: shaming yourself, or allowing others to shame you, will never actually help you get better. You can't shame yourself, or be shamed, into being more functional. It wasn't until Rich actually showed me how to properly make a bed, and stood with me the first few times so I could learn visually, that I started to be able to do it alone. He never laughed at me for being a thirty-something with no idea how to do this task that he found so incredibly simple, and he never questioned that it was a real struggle for me. He listened, and then helped me. I won't be working for a luxury five-star hotel any time soon, but I can make the bed most days, and it feels great. Compassion and non-judgement will bring about more positive change than shame and judgement ever will.

Rich will also share his real-life experiences of each of my symptoms. He'll tell you about his struggles with some of my behaviour before diagnosis, and the way he handles things now that he knows I have ADHD. I'll add here that he's also done a lot of research and work on how best to support a neurodivergent partner. My hope is that every neurodivergent person has someone who can care for them in this way. I cannot emphasise enough what his love has done to heal the deep wounds left by a lifetime of feeling like a failure.

Whether you are a partner, parent, or friend, we hope not only that you learn how best to support your ADHDer, but that you'll recognise that you, too, matter deeply: your own experiences, your emotions, your struggles. This is not simply a book about how to support an ADHD person. It's a book about understanding what it's truly like to love someone with ADHD, warts and all, and the tools we all can use to create a healthy and happy home for everyone affected by ADHD.

Whether you hyperfocus on this book and read it all in the next two hours, or whether it joins a mountain of unread books and you finally get round to skimming it in 2034 when you're moving house, we hope you find value in these pages. We hope you feel less alone. From the bottom of our hearts to yours, thank you for being here.

Rox and Rich

SYMPTOM ONE:
LOSING IMPORTANT THINGS

AKA "Babe, have you seen my wallet?"
Written by Rox

Over the course of my life, I have lost so many things. All of the classics: 13 phones, 18 wallets, two passports. That last one meant not only a missed holiday, but also a warning letter from Her Majesty the Queen herself. Passports are royal property. Who knew!? I can't tell you the number of times I've stood outside various homes that I have lived in, locked out, calling a locksmith, with my phone on 2 percent, wondering if there is enough money on my maxed-out credit card to get me inside. One night there wasn't, so I slept on my doorstep.

What would happen in my body, when I realised I had lost something important, was a powerful cocktail of stress and shame. My stomach would feel like it was falling out, I'd sense my face start to burn red, tears would be choking the back of my throat as I realised what I had done. Again. Every time I lost something important I chastised myself for my careless behaviour and stupidity, screaming at myself internally in the hopes that that would somehow stop me from losing things in the future. Of course... it didn't work.

I want to share with you the saddest thing I have ever lost. It was a letter written to me by my mum when she was dying. I have no idea where exactly I lost it, but it would have been during one of my many apartment moves in my twenties. I can barely describe the pain losing this letter caused me. I hated myself to my core for what I had done—for losing something so precious that I would never get back. My mum's last words to me. What a horrible, disgusting daughter I was. It wasn't until my ADHD diagnosis that I was able to begin to loosen the shackles of self-hatred.

The fact I lost that letter still brings tears to my eyes; it makes me so incredibly sad. But now, rather than screaming at myself internally, I take a deep breath, acknowledge the sadness, and offer compassion to myself.

I share this story as a way to scream to you, "*I don't mean to lose things!*" I feel I need to scream this, to prove to you how much it hurts to lose things and to make you understand that I really don't do it on purpose, because for the majority of my life people have rolled their eyes at me and called me careless, reckless, and disrespectful. So here I am, sharing my deepest pain with you, in the hopes you may forgive me for my sins. The sheer depth of misunderstanding and judgement others have shown me, and the callous way some people have treated me, has led me to some very dark places. I still have scars on my skin as reminders.

When I started to learn about ADHD, for the first time that crippling self-hatred and those desperate attempts to justify my forgetfulness started to soften. The narrative began to change, albeit slowly, from one of personal failure to one of self-understanding. *Wait,* I thought. *So I really was telling the truth? I really didn't mean to be so forgetful? There might be a reason for this?* It was like I had been choking my whole life, and suddenly I could breathe again. I was okay. Not broken. What I needed wasn't more judgement or scolding; what I needed was therapy, and a hell of a lot of compassion. That was the most powerful part of diagnosis for me: the removal of a lifetime of crippling shame.

Of course, a diagnosis isn't magic. It didn't suddenly turn me from the queen of self-loathing to a fully paid member of the "live, laugh, love" brigade. But I now had a different internal narrative when things went missing. A diagnosis doesn't mean that you stop losing things. I'm sober, I'm in a really supportive relationship, I've had some amazing therapy and … I still lose things regularly. In the last six months, for example, I've lost three wallets. The first, a beautiful engraved, lime-green one that Rich had bought me for Christmas, was lost somewhere in London Bridge Station. RIP. He was kind and understanding, and he bought me a replacement—which I lost a few weeks later somewhere in Kings Cross. RIP. Rich was kind and understanding yet again. That takes us to wallet number three. Strap in for this story.

I was on a train down to Brighton to meet Rich after work when a familiar feeling began to rise: *sheer panic.* At the train station gates, I began frantically searching through my pockets and my bag. My heart rate increased, my face got hot, and I could feel emotions bubbling as I realised I had lost yet another wallet. I broke down in tears and began struggling to catch my breath. I called Rich, who, in typical Rich fashion, was early and already waiting for me outside the station. In a very shaky voice, I explained what had happened. He calmed me down, came and found me, bought me a new ticket (in the UK you need to show your ticket to get *out* of a train station!), got me through the barriers and then hugged me for a solid 10 minutes while I cried into his shoulder saying *I'm so stupid, I'm so stupid* over and over again. He told me I wasn't, and reassured me for the millionth time that it was okay. Onlookers at Brighton probably thought we were breaking up. Little did they know this is just what life with ADHD can sometimes look like.

After I'd calmed down, Rich suggested that instead of buying expensive wallets, I should maybe have a cheaper one instead. He also suggested that he would keep hold of the majority of my cards and ID, so if I did lose my wallet again, I'd have only a bank card to replace. God bless this man. He never shouted at me; he never shamed me. He helped me process my shame, and then helped me with strategies to support me. As I write this book, I have not lost a wallet for four months. Call the Guinness Book of ADHD World Records!

SUGGESTIONS TO HELP

You've likely seen them all: the "ADHD check" when you leave a room, the sticky-notes on the doors reminding you what you need to take, the special pocket for your keys... The internet is full of practical strategies for how to stop losing things. Honestly, none of them worked for me. Maybe they would for a day, but soon I'd forget what I needed to be doing and not only was I still losing things, but I was then also feeling rubbish for not properly following all the tips! Double shame sandwich. No thank you.

So we're approaching this in a different way. *You have ADHD. You are going to lose things.* Let's just try and lose the slightly less important stuff. Acceptance is so often the key to actually feeling better. Accepting you will lose things means you are not fighting against yourself, or shaming yourself. You know what happens when we stop fighting and shaming ourselves? We actually do lose fewer things! Magic.

Here are some tried-and-tested tips that actually work:

DITCH THE SHAME: When you lose something, it feels absolutely horrible. Especially if the thing you lost was really important to you. The stress and guilt of losing the thing is enough pain. You do not need to punish or bully yourself. And no one around you should be doing that either. You didn't mean to lose this thing. You would have much preferred it if you hadn't, and it's a goddamn horrible feeling. So... No bullying. From anyone, including yourself. You have ADHD. You are going to lose things. It's okay. You are not a terrible person.

STRIVE TO REGULATE YOUR EMOTIONS: Losing something important can overwhelm you emotionally and make it feel like you can't cope. Symptoms similar to a panic attack are common for the overwhelmed ADHDer who has, for instance, just locked themselves out of their house. When you feel these big emotions coming up, use your breathing to calm yourself down. Breathe deeply from the belly, counting in for eight and out for eight, for as long as you need to. You'll feel your body start to calm down. Slow breaths signal to your nervous system that you are not in danger and will help regulate yourself. Then, when you feel a little calmer, you'll be able to bring some logic to the situation.

REDUCE STRESS: Stress makes ADHD symptoms worse. Be extra vigilant when you're starting to feel stressed or anxious. Running late for a train? This is a red alert that you might lose or forget something. Slow down, maybe try those breathing exercises from the paragraph above, and listen to your body. Notice what you are worried about, and take a little more time for yourself in these situations.

PUT SOME SAFETY NETS IN PLACE: Give a neighbour a spare key, keep a spare SIM card, carry a portable phone charger, pay that £10 a month for phone insurance, leave your ID at home if you don't need it, and leave expensive things at home if you can. Streamline the things you need to remember so that when you do lose something, it's from the less important list.

"It's okay. I'll cancel your cards."
Written by Rich

Since Rox and I have been together, which is four years at the time we're writing this book, she has lost nine pairs of headphones. Eight of these were those £30 iPhone headphones, which is not so bad. But one set were the £250 noise-cancelling headphones I bought her for Christmas. Ouch.

At first, when Rox lost something, particularly if it was a gift, or something that belonged to me, it would really upset me. *Surely if she cared about me*, I'd mutter to myself, *she would be more careful with these things?* I used to get really annoyed, and although I'd try and hide it, she's a mind-Jedi in terms of reading my emotions, and she would know. So picture the scene: she's just told me she's lost the expensive headphones I bought her. Her hands and voice are shaking, she's red in the face, and she's obviously very ashamed. I feel the anger boiling inside me, as I can't believe this has happened again; it really feels like she is doing this on purpose. We are both feeling lonely and misunderstood. Just FYI, this is a situation we found ourselves in many times before she got her diagnosis.

You see, for me, taking care of things comes pretty easily. I've got a good memory, I'm organised, and knowing where important items are at all times is basically burned into the back of my brain. If I were to constantly lose things, it would mean I was actually doing it on purpose. Perhaps I'd lose things to hurt someone, or because I had no respect for these items. That was the only explanation that made sense to me—the sheer amount of losing that Rox was doing meant there must be some malice behind it. Because that is how *my* brain works.

And that's the kicker. *My brain.* It's very different to her brain. And projecting my way of living in this world onto her was extremely unfair. Our brains are very different: something I find really easy, she finds terribly hard. Bottom line: if someone is struggling with something, anger and frustration certainly won't help them get better.

When Rox got her diagnosis, and we both began to realise the reason why she struggles so much with losing things, not only did it help her enormously with shame removal, but it also really helped me! Now I understood that she didn't lose things because she didn't care about me, or to upset me; she lost things because she has ADHD. Suddenly we were both on the same team, working toward the same goal: how could we support each other through this? How could we help each other be happier? It was no longer me against Rox losing things. It was me and Rox against a symptom of ADHD.

Since then, I have worked hard to not react with frustration or anger when she inevitably loses something. It's taken practice and patience, but I'm proud to say that I'm now at the point where my natural reaction is warmth and compassion. I have a new system in my head that works. First, I lean in to kindness and emotional regulation. Rox is often very stressed and dysregulated when she has lost something. I tell her it's okay, I hug her, and I encourage her to breathe. Second, when I can feel she's returned to a calm state, I help her with the practical parts of this loss. It may involve cancelling cards, or phoning a restaurant to see if the thing she's lost is still there. These are things I find easy, that I know how to do, but for her they can feel impossible.

That doesn't mean that my emotions go unheard, though. I will let Rox know if losing something I've bought her has hurt me, but I will do it with kindness, and I will only share this after she has calmed down and we've done the practical steps. It might sound like this: "I'm not gonna lie—I'm a bit upset you lost the wallet I bought you, but I know you didn't do it on purpose and that it's ADHD." She will always apologise to me, cuddle me, and reassure me.

We have created an environment of safety, so Rox knows she can ring me the moment she has lost something. This means I can help her and she doesn't have to suffer alone. There is no shame in our household now when she loses something—and I genuinely believe this has helped her lose fewer things. She has had one wallet for four months now, for example, and I'm really proud of her.

SUPPORTING AN ADHDer WHO LOSES THINGS

Here's the thing: as we said earlier, your ADHDer is going to lose things. And trust me, they are already going to feel awful about it. The suggestions we'll give you below aren't to stop them losing things. Rather, they'll help you support them in a kind and compassionate way, while also making sure you are looked after. I have witnessed first-hand how accepting your ADHDer as someone who loses things, and supporting them every time it happens, can actually help them lose fewer things.

DON'T GET ANGRY: Your ADHDer will be feeling bad enough; you don't need to add to it. Yes, you can feel annoyed, but practice reaching for kindness in the moment. They will likely be feeling incredibly lost and ashamed at first, and they need you to show them it's okay. Afterwards, when they have calmed down, you can share with them your experience and allow them to comfort you. Trying to reason with someone who is triggered will only hurt both of you.

AIM FOR CO-REGULATION: Calming your ADHDer down after they have lost something is the first task, whether that's a phone call to reassure them that everything will be okay, or hugging them as they cry over losing another phone. Just being there for them, calmly and kindly, is enough to move them through these overwhelming emotions.

HELP WITH THE PRACTICALITIES: If you're neurotypical, your practical skills are like gold dust to your ADHDer. When ADHD strikes, can you help them cancel their cards, sort out an insurance claim, or call a lost property department? Giving assistance in these areas is one of the best ways you can help an ADHDer.

WORK ON A SOLUTION TOGETHER: Chat to your ADHDer about their pattern of losing things. Come up with strategies together that help mitigate the losses. Do they need to take their ID out of their wallet every day? Can you keep a spare key somewhere? Is there a drawer you can put that important letter in? Working together against the symptom, as opposed to working against each other, will help you both feel happier and more supported.

SYMPTOM TWO: TIME BLINDNESS

AKA "I'll be ready in five minutes!"
Written by Rox

Ninety-nine percent of the time I'm running late. This is not a metaphor. You will very often find me running through London Bridge Station, oat milk latte in one hand, phone in the other, sweating profusely as I wonder if it's best to lie, or to tell the truth about why I'm not on time. I compose a text in my head:

Sorry I'm late—I sat on my bed staring at the window for 25 minutes for no particular reason.

I would actually love to be able to send a text like that. It's giving, authentic, human, and real. But something tells me the important music manager I'm on my way to meet might not agree. I settle for a classic:

Sorry I'm late. Trains were awful this morning.

You can always rely on UK trains to be unreliable; in this sense, they're an excellent source for ADHD excuse generation.

But it's not only trains I am late for. Oh no—it's EVERYTHING. It's work, doctors' appointments, and flights. Once in 2017 I missed a flight from London to LA due to what I call my Google Maps time optimism, leaving at the last possible moment and never taking into account traffic or delays! I was extremely lucky that the understanding lady behind the British Airways desk took pity on me and rebooked me *for free* on a flight later that day. I couldn't believe my luck. What a near miss!

I took a seat in the departure lounge, all the while sending up a prayer of gratitude to the BA gods. I had four hours to wait, but I stayed put: I knew if I left the airport I would run the risk of being late again. (Look at me being *sensible!*) So I found a chair near the gate and waited. And waited. I waited so long, in fact, that when I went to go through security I was greeted with an error code. The staff informed me that I had missed the one-hour minimum time window to enter security. I stood there staring at them, part bemused (Surely this cannot be real… surely I am dreaming and this is a comedy) and part petrified (What the hell do I do now??). That nice lady had already rebooked me for free… How was I going to I tell her I'd missed THIS flight too?! What on earth was she going to think of me??

For the second time that day, I revisited the British Airways desk. I approached my guardian angel and told her I had missed my flight, yet again with no possible reason or excuse, other than that time had slipped away from me. I didn't have an ADHD diagnosis at the time, and I was incredibly confused and upset by my own behaviour. I started crying. "I'm so sorry. I'm an absolute idiot. I don't know how I've done this."

To my astonishment, she started laughing. "Oh, sweetheart, what a day you have had," she said. She pushed a few buttons on her keyboard. "You're rebooked for tomorrow. Please set an alarm." Third time lucky, I thought as I boarded my transatlantic flight the following day.

I don't like being late. In fact, I HATE it. Whether it's leaving the house a sweaty, forgetful mess, or having to tell my brother I'll be arriving tomorrow because I missed my flight, I hate, hate, *hate* it. It makes me feel incredibly ashamed and terribly anxious. So, if I hate it so much, I would ask myself, why can't I just be on time? This question baffled me for years. I'd tried everything: setting two alarms, planning out my routes, leaving early. No matter what I did, though, it's like the universe would bend and shift around me to make me late.

Oh, you think you're on time? Lol. I've just cancelled your train.

A flight in one hour? Oh dear… look at the seismic queue at security.

I ran late for thirty years. Think about that:

Thirty years of excuses.

Thirty years of hating myself.

Thirty years of not understanding why I couldn't just sort it out.

Thirty years of people getting very annoyed with me.

I've also lost so much money on missed trains, missed appointments, and of course missed flights. The ADHD tax is very real. And worse, I've no doubt made many friends and colleagues feel like I don't respect them, or their time, as I arrive flustered once again, with some half-baked excuse about trains.

It's no wonder that when I first read the term "time blindness," I felt understood for the first time in decades. Being late is a symptom of ADHD. It's part of my difficulty in living in a world that depends on time… Time blindness is something that makes sense to me—and like loads of other ADHD symptoms, this too can be supported. I'll show you how in a moment.

Time blindness could quite easily be called time optimism. For example, let's say I need to leave my house in 45 minutes for an appointment, and there is an episode I want to watch on Netflix that's one hour long. I genuinely believe that I can make this work—that somehow the episode will play a bit quicker, that time itself will bend to allow me to leave the house at my desired time. I'm basically a time wizard. Only my magic does not work.

Despite ample evidence to the contrary, the curse of time optimism never goes away.

"How long do you need to get ready?" Rich will ask me.

"Five minutes," I say confidently.

Forty-five minutes later I emerge, finally ready to leave, and he is more than a bit annoyed. I don't understand.

For me, five minutes and 45 minutes mean the exact same thing.

They mean "not now, but soon."

You see, I don't work in time. I work in either "right now" or "in a bit."

Five minutes means "not now," the same way that 45 minutes means "not now."

The only time that can be trusted is *right now*.

Since my ADHD diagnosis, I have gotten a *little* better with time management. I'm by no means perfect, but armed with the knowledge that I believe I am a magical time wizard, I can call myself out on my own absurdity. For instance, as I go to text Rich that "I'll be home in 15 mins" when I know full well I am on a train journey that takes an hour, I call out my time wizardry, delete the text, and type in something more accurate. I'm unlearning a lifetime of lying about time, of trying desperately to conceal my shame and only making it worse. It's only by being honest that we can begin to accept these parts of ourselves, and allow others to accept them too.

I'd like to take credit for not missing any flights recently, but I can't help but feel that Rich, Mr. "We must arrive at the airport three hours before departure," may deserve a little more of that credit. What I can take credit for is being honest with people. I'll let people know in advance I struggle with ADHD and am often late. As soon as they say "Thanks for telling me. No problem," it's like this huge pressure to get it right has been lifted and I am way more likely to be on time. I also do plan a lot better; I look for where my time optimism is showing up, and try and build it into my plans. It isn't perfect. Or magic. But it is progress. And I'm happy with that.

SUGGESTIONS TO HELP

I'm not going to tell you to set five alarms, tell Alexa about your appointments, or always leave an hour earlier. These things are temporary. And an uphill battle. I have something bigger to ask of you: to accept that you struggle with time, and are very often late.

"What, *what*?!" I hear you saying. "This crazy blue-haired lady is telling me it's okay to just be late all the time?!" No. That's not what I'm saying. It isn't okay. It can upset people, and it can cause you, yourself, a lot of stress. What I'm saying is, let's start from acceptance. I'm saying that time is a really difficult concept for you, and let's try and make it a little easier.

USE RADICAL ACCEPTANCE: I have some bad news. Time doesn't work normally for you. In your mind, it's either right now or some unidentified point in the future. Those are the only two times you have. And your relentless optimism that time itself will magically change for you isn't going to go away. But knowing that this is how your brain perceives time will really help. You're a time wizard with faulty magic. So, let's try and get you operating in a non-magic world.

TELL THE TRUTH: Practise being incredibly honest. For example, if you are already late to a meeting, and Uber says you are 15 minutes away, your text saying "I'll be there in 8 minutes" is going to make your life worse. Yes, shaving off that little chunk of time might make you feel less ashamed in the moment, but in the long run it will tie you up in knots of anxiety as time fails once more to bend to your needs. So, when you tell people why you are running late, *tell the truth*. A genuine "I'm so sorry. Time ran away with me this morning" carries authenticity. It's a lot less stressful to tell the truth than it is to lie—and it involves a hell of a lot less sweating!

MAKE A JOKE OUT OF IT: Don't present yourself as someone who is good with time. I know it's hard to accept personal failings. But the more you fight it, the more you try and hide it behind excuses like "the trains were running late," the harder life will be. Have a laugh with those close to you about the fact that you're always running late. Share with them in a light-hearted way that you struggle with this, rather than keeping it as some dark, shameful secret. Putting your struggles out in the open helps remove the shame. It takes a lot of mental energy to hide this behaviour; sharing your "dark secret" and poking a bit of fun at it will actually free up brain power to help you be on time. Now, that does sound a little like magic, doesn't it?

BUILD NEW HABITS: I have a challenge for you to work on. Knowing you think you can actually bend time, I want you to start to pre-plan your journeys, especially the important ones. There is no guesstimating allowed. You must always allow a buffer for unexpected delays. And you must always *over*-estimate how long it will take you to get from Point A to Point B. As you practise these skills, you'll get better at them—I promise. It will take time and effort, but as you start to learn you aren't absolutely useless with time, you will build self-esteem and confidence in this area. And—you guessed it—people with more confidence around time tend to be more on time.

"Is that a real five minutes? Or an ADHD five minutes?"
Written by Rich

I'm sat downstairs staring at my watch. Rox said she would be ready five minutes ago. Forty minutes have gone by. We've already missed the high-intensity interval training (HIIT) class we were booked in for. I can feel my anger levels rising. It feels like she is doing this intentionally to wind me up. There's no other explanation. I walk upstairs, hitting every step a little harder than usual, taking out my frustrations. I walk into Rox's office.

There she is.

Headphones on.

Singing.

Absolutely oblivious to the chaos she is causing.

"BABE!" I say loudly.

She jumps and turns around. A look of panic comes over her face.

"I've been waiting for you for over 40 minutes. We've missed the gym class now."

She looks genuinely shocked. Apologises profusely and jumps up from what she's doing, in a mad rush to find her gym gear. As if moving at light speed in this moment will somehow reverse time and we'll still make the class.

When we'd both calmed down, we had a conversation about her lateness. Her explanation for why we missed the class?

I just didn't look at the time.

I genuinely thought I would only be five minutes.

This was our first argument. No voices were raised—we've done too much therapy for that. But we were annoyed with each other, both feeling misunderstood and alone. Without Rox's ADHD diagnosis, which was to come a few months later, I now wonder if arguments like this could have eventually torn us apart.

Being on time is really important for me. Whether its's the big stuff, like catching flights and being on time for work meetings, or the small stuff, like getting to a gym class, I like to be punctual, even early. Time helps me structure my day, and lateness is a quality that I don't like in people. It feels disorganised at best, highly disrespectful at worst. And here I was, in love with somebody who was perpetually late. Ironically, it's one of the most reliable things about Rox.

When Rox got her diagnosis, and we found the term "time blindness" after many hours of Googling and watching TikToks, it was a game changer for us. She was able to explain, and I was able to understand, that she really struggles with the concept of time. Not because she's being disrespectful, or because she doesn't care—in fact, I can see the mess she gets in when she is running late: nobody would choose this. It was affecting her life negatively, just as much as it was affecting mine. Once again, rather than me versus Rox, we became Rox and me versus time blindness.

For me, believing Rox when she says she'll be five minutes, or allowing her to catch a train I know won't get her to her destination on time, feels like setting her up to fail. And that's where I had been: setting little time goals and watching, almost expectantly, as she failed again, then taking that as evidence she didn't love me. When I broke through that, when I realised she was honestly trying her best but found punctuality incredibly difficult, I was able to support her in ways that have completely changed her time-keeping. She's gotten a lot better. How? By accepting she doesn't understand time, and by letting me help her.

Now, when Rox says she needs "five minutes…"

I say, "Is that an ADHD five minutes? Or shall we just say an hour?"

When Rox says it will take her an hour to get to London…

I say, "Does that include getting ready to leave and a safety margin if the trains are late?"

When Rox says "It's absolutely fine getting to the airport one hour before a flight…"

I say, "Babe… I have never missed a flight. You missed two in one day. Trust me on this one."

We laugh a lot about our different interpretations of time. But now, she leans on me when she needs help, and I'll call her out when time blindness is getting in the way. I've stopped moralising time-keeping as something that makes a person good or bad, and she has really tried to get better with time management. She hasn't missed a train in months. And that achievement is something to be celebrated. Treating Rox's time-related struggles with understanding, compassion and humour has not only made us both happier, but it has really helped her develop better time-keeping skills. Like most things, time-keeping is a skill that needs understanding and then practising. Creating a safe environment for your ADHDer to do that can be a game changer.

SUPPORTING AN ADHDer WITH TIME BLINDNESS

Your ADHDer thinks they are a time wizard who can bend the space–time continuum if they are running late. Think of them like Harry Potter, pointing his wand at a queue of traffic and shouting "Punctualis!"—and then realising his magic isn't working. Only Harry never loses his belief that one day his spell will work. That's what you're dealing with. Your ADHDer does not see time in the way that you do, so trying to force them to see life through your lens just won't work.

Like so many of the ADHD symptoms, being late is only ever exacerbated by stress! A lifetime of running late and using faulty magic often means your ADHDer is highly stressed out when leaving to get somewhere important. Helping them to be less stressed is the best way to help them get better with time. So that's what we're going to focus on.

CHANGE THE NARRATIVE: If your ADHDer is always running late, realise it's because they struggle with it, not because they don't love or respect you. Of course it can be frustrating when someone is late, and you can explain that calmly and kindly when any mad rush is over. But supporting better time management skills will give you much better results than shaming and arguments ever will. This is a problem for you both to solve, rather than an issue for you to argue about.

DON'T SET THEM UP TO FAIL: Don't ask what time your ADHDer will be home, and then sit in victorious annoyance as they walk through the door two hours late. Rather, when they give you a time, say something like, "There are no expectations for you to make this time. Let me know if you need any help planning the journey." Paradoxically, removing the pressure can actually help them be more on time! However, if there is a really important event you need them to be ready for—for example, catching a flight—give your ADHDer plenty of notice, and support them in their efforts.

USE TIME CHECK-INS: Friendly check-ins with your ADHDer to see how they are getting on when you have somewhere to be can act as a reminder to them, just in case whatever you have to do has slipped their mind. It's a great opportunity to double-check plans and support them if they have forgotten the event, and also helps them build a habit of thinking consciously about time. Developing this skill also increases their independence and confidence.

BE A TIME REALIST: When your ADHDer's magical time thinking is at work, call them back into reality. When they say it will take them only 20 minutes to walk to the doctor's, which you know is at least a 15-minute drive away, call it out. If possible, use humour so your reminder doesn't appear shaming or patronising: "Unless you are literally faster than Usain Bolt, that's not happening. Would you like a lift to the doctor's? No? Okay, if you want to walk, you are going to need to leave an hour earlier." The more you can reflect reality back to them, the more their brain will start to grasp how time actually works.

SYMPTOM THREE: HYPERFOCUS

AKA "Gimme five hours to research that real quick!"

Attention Deficit Hyperactivity Disorder. Attention... deficit? Man... Whoever came up with that name got things completely wrong.

I do not have a deficit of attention.

I have a wild, untameable attention. It doesn't like focusing on the simple, the easy, or the mundane. My attention loves challenge, novelty, and unfortunately, it thrives on stress.

Let me introduce you to my superpower, which isn't really a superpower because I have no control over how I use it (imagine if Superman started to fly when he was trying to sleep). My superpower is *hyperfocus*.

Hyperfocus is to blame for my being labelled a "gifted kid" by my parents and teachers growing up. I have zero blame or resentment for them, mind you; ADHD wasn't really known about in the '80s. Throughout my junior school years, I would become obsessed with certain subjects. For example, Egypt. I memorised history books, learned incredibly obscure facts, asked to be taken to museums, and made PowerPoint presentations crammed with all my knowledge. I couldn't go a day without telling somebody that a *shadoof* was an ancient Egyptian irrigation device. If they seemed interested, I'd also offer to show them the real-life working model I had constructed from clay. Those around me looked at my passion and thirst for knowledge and said, "Genius! Sign her up to Mensa." News flash: my passion for Egypt wasn't actually due to being gifted; it was due to undiagnosed ADHD and the fact my brain had decided to hyperfocus on that particular topic.

In reality, I really struggled to focus in class, stay up to date with homework, and work in any resemblance of a healthy way. I could only truly focus when my brain made a particular school subject into an obsession. Those obsessional periods of work would be highly praised by those around me, and I absorbed the compliments about my work ethic and intelligence. Sure, my bedroom was a disgusting mess, and I could never arrive anywhere on time, but I was a gifted child, right? So I figured this must just be how gifted children operate.

But take the incorrectly labelled gifted child, put them in the real world, and guess what happens? A crushing sense of personal failure, of not living up to one's oh-so-incredible potential, followed by a barrage of mental health issues stemming from plummeting self-esteem. Looking back now, watching my 11-year-old self marching proudly to my extra maths class at school, I just want to scream "STOP! Somebody please show this kid how to regulate her nervous system, how to make her bed, how to take care of herself. And while you're at it, tell her she doesn't need to be gifted to be loved. That she's enough, just as she is."

After entering adult life, armed only with the knowledge that I was gifted and thus destined for great things, I set about trying to find employment. My first post-university job? Training to be an accountant. "Gifted kid heaven," I thought. "Let's go!" Three months into the course, however, I was utterly overwhelmed by the workload, unable to cope like my peers seemed to be doing, and questioning my entire identity. *I am meant to find schoolwork easy. So the problem can't be me. I'm a genius. This course must just not be right.* In the end, I quit.

On to job number two: training to be a trader in the city. Fast paced, well paid, and surrounded by incredibly smart people. Finally, this felt like home. I passed my exams with flying colours, the only junior trader on the desk to pass everything first time around. This was not because I had understood anything, mind you, but because I had memorised the textbooks the night before the exams. I was promoted quickly and soon dealing with multi-million-pound trades over the phone. Imposter syndrome and anxiety hit like a ton of bricks. I'd often forget what I was told, write things down incorrectly, and miss a trade when my brain was not working quickly enough. The familiar shame kicked in: *I am supposed to be a genius. Why am I struggling?*

I'll tell you why. Because my ability to hyperfocus, to impress teachers with my knowledge of ancient Egypt, and to pass financial exams first time round had me and everybody else convinced I was meant to succeed in a *neurotypical world*. Neurotypical success looks like this: a high-paying corporate job, stability, promotions, benefits, and a long and prosperous career. In reality, I was the total opposite of someone who would succeed in that kind of environment. I was disorganised, impulsive, and highly creative. But my identity, my self-esteem, and in some way my destiny, were so tied to external success I had no choice but to keep pursuing the excellence that always evaded me. I had to find a way to be exceptional in this world, or else... who was I? Being gifted was the only thing I liked about myself, and the only thing the outside world liked about me. Without it? I was nothing. I've spent many hours in therapy in my adult life unpacking this particular thought...

Things are very different now. If I watch *Bohemian Rhapsody* and start hyperfocusing on Freddie Mercury, reading all the books about him and learning all the facts, nobody around me calls me a genius and packs me off for a fast-track PhD in Queen studies. I am just allowed to spend hours down that rabbit hole until it's no longer making me happy, and then await the next dopamine-inducing obsession. That's how it should be. Hyperfocus is an extremely intense ability to focus on a particular subject, for a duration of time that cannot be estimated. It appears on a whim, and turns off whenever it chooses. It is absolutely not the thing on which to base one's identity and future life choices.

But since my diagnosis, and learning to understand the symptom, I have found it to have some useful applications! For instance, any time Rich and I are going on holiday, I *have* to spend hours reading about our destination, researching it, and memorising every hotel option. I can easily sit on my phone for five hours doing all this work, guided by the notion that I am going to find the *absolute best* place to stay. I suppose you could say this is the tale of a former gifted child trying to book an adult holiday. I *must* make the best choice; I *will* get an A in holiday planning! Due to this, we've ended up enjoying some pretty incredible experiences together.

My hyperfocus is just something Rich and I have accepted as part of our lives together. It often kicks in after watching a film, seeing a new crafting hobby on Pinterest, or hearing something on the news that I need to know more about. He'll know when I'm about to enter my research zone and give me space to do it. He'll also make sure I have a drink and something to eat, just like when I'm doing "holiday research," as I get so engrossed in what I'm doing I forget both these things! We both know I'll wear myself out eventually, leaving the hyperfocus rabbit hole with some new knowledge, a purchase, or perhaps a new hobby. If I could control my hyperfocus I'd be unstoppable, but luckily for the *real* kid geniuses out there, that is never going to happen.

SUGGESTIONS TO HELP

Do you have the sense that if you could just control your hyperfocus, you'd be unstoppable? I imagine many ADHDers feel this way. We read books on focus and discipline, and we try our hardest to change. What happens? We fail epically. We feel more shame. And we end up in a worse situation that we were in before. No thanks.

You can't control your periods of hyperfocus. All you can do is accept them, work with them, and allow them to *just be*. You don't need to take this part of yourself and beat it within an inch of its life, trying to force it to work to make you successful in a neurotypical world. It's time to let hyperfocus just be a thing that you do, rather than something that must be tamed in order for you to feel lovable.

IF YOU ARE/WERE A GIFTED CHILD: Were you labelled a gifted child? Do you live with a crazy amount of pressure to live up to the potential everyone told you you had? It's time to redefine yourself. It's possible you're not a gifted child, but rather a child (or adult) with ADHD. ADHD can present as giftedness. It can also appear to be a disability. It's important to see both sides of it. You don't have to be excellent, super-intelligent, or highly creative to be worthy of love and respect.

LANGUAGE MATTERS: You aren't being crazy, lazy, or obsessive when you are researching something avidly. You are hyperfocusing.

Using the correct language takes the shame out of the experience, and lets those around you know what's happening. Being able to label yourself as being in *hyperfocus mode* means you get to enjoy those hours. You get to have drinks and snacks, and let yourself just be you.

BEWARE OF BURNOUT: Hours spent researching a topic or studying for an exam can lead to burnout. You might be your happiest, most focused ever, reading every IMDB review out there to decide what film to watch tonight, but after a certain amount of time, your brain will have had enough. Sustained periods of hyperfocus can take you from crazy levels of excitement to numbness and despair really quickly. There's nothing wrong with you; it's just exhausting to focus so hard on one thing. Take a break, have a cuddle, be kind to yourself. You can always go back to the task another day.

RIDE THE WAVE: Hyperfocus can have you starting a new business, moving to a new country, or deciding you need a career change on a whim. My advice? Do the research, dream the dream, but *don't act yet*. Making decisions in the middle of hyperfocus can be destructive; your decisions will probably be poorly thought out, not to mention expensive. Allow your brain to wander wherever it needs to go, but keep it under control. Don't allow it to press "self-destruct." If an idea has been persistent for a long time, and there are sensible reasons to do it, then you can revisit making big decisions based on that idea from a calmer state. For me, most of the time after I've ridden the current hyperfocus wave, I'm perfectly happy to leave it there.

An important side note: *occasionally*, following an idea that comes to you in a time of hyperfocus can be an incredible decision. It would be wrong of me not to mention that my hyperfocus on creating ADHD TikTok content is why you are holding this book in your hands. But for the most part, just ride the wave and hold off on huge decisions until you've had time to calm down and maybe bounce them off someone supportive.

"Looks like you are going into hyperfocus mode… I'll get you a drink"
Written by Rich

I book a hotel in 10 minutes. Here's my process.

1. Visit booking.com.
2. Search where and when we're travelling.
3. Click on the first one that's got a decent price and a few good reviews.
4. Book.

Simple. Efficient. Right?

My wife's hotel booking process? A complex research project, consisting of many open Safari tabs, in-depth review and analysis, and photo comparison. What it *doesn't* seem to consist of is any awareness whatsoever about our budget. Let me share a story with you:

I look over at Rox's phone and can see she is looking at a hotel that costs £1000 a night. Honestly, it's infuriating. I just want to get this booked as soon as possible, and we certainly don't have the budget of a millionaire!

"Can you at least just look at realistic options? This feels like a massive waste of time," I tell her.

If you *don't* want a conversation to go well, start it this way. Works every time. Rox ended up walking out of the room, visibly upset.

Later, over dinner, Rox explained something to me that has changed how we deal with her hyperfocus.

"I'll never ask to book the thousand-pound-per-night hotel. It just makes me really happy to know all the details of all the available options. It's really fun for me, and if I don't get to do that I feel sad, anxious, and like I've missed out on something."

For the first time, I really started to understand this behaviour: she wasn't looking to recklessly spend money or waste time. No, for her this was a research project. And she wanted to do a really good job. Knowing the extreme options allowed her to judge the value of the more realistic ones, with the ultimate goal of finding us somewhere really special, for the best price.

Whenever Rox is hyperfocusing these days, whether it's booking a hotel, researching Freddie Mercury after watching *Bohemian Rhapsody*, or deep-diving into her latest favourite psychology podcast, we both know what's happening. I'll check in with her occasionally to make sure she's not burning out, and offer to get her drinks and snacks while she descends into her latest obsession.

SUPPORTING AN ADHDer WITH HYPERFOCUS

Watching your ADHDer disappear down a hyperfocus rabbit hole is going to be part of life. Trying to stop it, limit it, or, even worse, focus it in a *productive* way will be really difficult for both of you. They have likely spent their whole life struggling to get control over this superpower, feeling like if they could, perhaps they could lead a happier and more successful life. We don't want to add to that.

Just like some people enjoy going for a walk or watching a movie, an

ADHDer can enjoy intensely researching various topics. Allowing them to just do this, with no judgement or pressure, can help them to accept this as part of who they are, rather than something they need to learn to control.

COMMUNICATE: Figure out what your ADHDer likes to focus on, and create space for it. This might sound like "Would you like a couple of hours to research where we're going for dinner tonight?" Then, simply leave them to it. Let their wonderful brains dive into a world of research and possibilities, and hopefully you'll end up somewhere absolutely awesome! If there is a time deadline, communicate it clearly.

SHARED JOY: Getting frustrated at your ADHDer when they excitedly show you a hotel with a swim-up bar and in-room masseuse ultimately hurts both of you. Instead, lean into the shared excitement about discovering something incredible, eye-catching, or odd, and take a moment to appreciate it with them. Being with them in their wonderful world is such a great way to reinforce that how they work is absolutely awesome.

BOUNDARIES: Whether it's a budget for a hotel or a time you need to leave for the cinema, clear boundaries will help your ADHDer work within the parameters. If they believe all options are available to them and then fall in love with a particular hotel or film, it can feel really disappointing to them if it doesn't happen. A clear boundary from you might sound like this: "I'm going leave you to focus on what film we watch tonight. Just a reminder: we have to leave by six thirty, so that's how long you've got."

KIND INTERRUPTIONS: If you see that wide-eyed look of excitement on your ADHDer's face start to fade into overwhelm and numbness, kindly suggest they take a break. Have a hug, or suggest they have a hot bath or a cup of tea. They can find it hard to detach from a research project if they don't feel they have completed it, and this can lead to burnout. So, friendly reminders for time-outs can be really helpful.

SYMPTOM FOUR:
POOR PERSONAL HYGIENE

AKA "Babe, do I smell of BO?"
Written by Rox

Imagine a "How to Know You've Met the One" article in some glossy women's magazine. He buys you flowers, sends good-morning texts, gets on with your family, right? Yeah, well, maybe that's a neurotypical list. However, if I were to write an article like that, it would sound ever so slightly different:

How to know you've met the one: He sniffs the armpits of your bodysuits to decide if they need an extra soak in the sink before washing them, due to your absolutely feral BO.

That's how you know it's true love.

I struggled with personal hygiene from the time I left home at 18 into my early 30s. I've never had a solid period of cleaning my teeth twice a day, and even if I had the motivation to do that, the toothpaste would run out and I wouldn't have a replacement, so my functional adult plans would be ruined.

I can imagine ADHDers reading this, nodding along and thinking, "OMG, that's me!" As for neurotypicals, I can imagine you might think this is all pretty gross. It's so hard to explain why a basic, simple task like a daily shower is such a struggle for me. I truly wish it wasn't. I've constantly felt embarrassed and dirty, relying on dry shampoo and Febreeze to get me through a day in functional society.

I want to share a pretty harrowing memory I have on this subject. When I was 23 I had a job working in the city of London for a posh investment bank. As you can imagine, the dress code was strict. Most days I would grab a skirt and top from the clothes on my floor (lovingly named my floordrobe), Febreeze them and myself, and head into work.

One day, a guy who sat next to me at work started saying, "What's that smell?"—with a pretty disgusted look on his face.

I cannot tell you the shame of sitting there realising that it was me. The floordrobe and Febreeze combo had stopped working. The bacteria had obviously overgrown my attempts to cover it. I went to the bathroom, washed my armpits, and put some hand wash on my clothes. My face burning red, I returned to my desk and waited for the clock to hit five so I could leave.

For many years of my life, I probably showered once every 10 days, and that would be because my head had started itching or I was going out to meet someone I liked. I just couldn't get on top of staying clean. Brushing my hair, cleaning my teeth and showering every day felt extremely overwhelming for me. My hair was regularly matted, and I have numerous fillings in my teeth from cavities I acquired during those years.

A decade later in my 30s, with an ADHD diagnosis in hand, a healthier, sober lifestyle and some great therapy, it's still pretty difficult for me. My outlook these days is "Two out of three ain't bad." I'm never going to bed showered, with brushed teeth and clean PJs, but I manage two of those things most days and that's good enough for me. Plus, I have an amazing partner who will do a BO check before I leave the house to help me avoid embarrassing moments.

SUGGESTIONS TO HELP

People without ADHD will often be showered, with clean teeth and clean clothes, *every day*. Seriously, how do these people find the time?! For us, that's almost impossible—unless meeting cleanliness standards becomes a full-time job, and let's be honest, we have far too many creative ventures we need to be working on. So, what do we do? We use dry shampoo, wear the same bra for three weeks straight, and feel absolutely disgusted at our ourselves.

It's time to change the rules. It's time to stop trying to be perfect. We have been set up to fail by societal standards that never took neurodiversity into consideration. So... here's a BO-friendly affirmation that I want you to marinate in: "I DO NOT NEED TO BE CLEAN TO BE LOVED." Yes, we feel great after a bath. No, we don't want to smell of BO at work. Yes, we understand being clean is a good thing. But it is not our life's purpose, and it is not a moral failing if we aren't. The only thing we need to be washing away daily is that shame we have covered ourselves in our whole lives.

SHAME REDUCTION: You are not disgusting or worthless if you struggle with personal hygiene. ADHDers often find this harder, and that's okay. So, let's focus on supporting you getting a little bit better. Believing that you are in some way broken or disgusting only makes it harder for you to take care of yourself. Self-care starts with being kind in the words you use about yourself. No more bullying on this topic, please.

WEAR-AGAIN SHELF: Keeping all of your clothes on the floor means they are going to smell and clutter up your space. It might feel like a victory, energy-wise, to leave your clothes wherever they fall, but in the long run you're making life so much harder for yourself. We have a wear-again shelf in our bedroom: it's a place for clothes that aren't ready to wash yet. It keeps them off the floor, so they stay cleaner and the bedroom is tidier. It's been a game changer.

PROGRESS, NOT PERFECTION: You aren't going to turn into a self-care guru overnight. It's likely that personal hygiene will continue to be a bit of a struggle. And that's okay. We're looking for progress, not perfection. Could you aim to clean your teeth once a day? How about showering every three days rather than once a week? Start with small, manageable changes, and that will help you set yourself up for success.

HONESTY: Trying to convince the world you are a showered, clean-toothed, functioning member of society on a daily basis is draining. You don't need to lie about it—at least not to those people who love you and that you feel safe with. Let these people know what you struggle with; sharing your challenges can really help reduce the shame. You can use humour about your slightly odd habits, and allow people to love you just as you are.

"Babe… I love you more than life itself. But you REALLY need a shower"
Written by Rich

It was drummed into my head as a child to have a shower every single morning and clean my teeth without fail. It's a forever habit, something I have never struggled with. I thought everybody was like me, until I met Rox.

When Rox first told me that she struggled with personal hygiene, I could hear the shame in her voice. Almost as if she felt I was going to end things with her, or at least tell her off. I remember feeling so sorry for her, and just wanting to hug her.

Before Rox's diagnosis, the only way she could describe her struggles with hygiene were with words like *lazy*, *disgusting*, and *gross*. It was clear she had lived so many years secretly hiding the way she existed from everyone because she saw it as something simply unlovable.

Even before her diagnosis, this was something we viewed with a lot of compassion. As we grew closer, and she felt safer, we'd even start joking about the last time she'd showered, or when she was going to change out of her favourite Misfits jumper.

The diagnosis, though? It changed everything. Suddenly she wasn't this deficient human incapable of looking after herself and unworthy of love. Rather, she was someone with ADHD who struggled with basic tasks, one of which is personal hygiene.

Something magic happens when a person suddenly has an explanation for their struggles, and language to describe them. The heaviness of shame, and the burden of keeping it from the world, is lifted. Rather than trying to be the cleanest person in the world and bullying herself for not meeting that standard, Rox now just accepts that personal hygiene is a struggle. The aim is to be good enough in a way that works for her.

Rox loves wearing nylon bodysuits. They're very cool for her edgy alt-girl look, but very bad for underarm BO due to the synthetic material. I take care of most of the washing in our house, and I noticed that even after a 40-degree wash, these bodysuits were *still smelling*. So, I came up with a BO-beating strategy. I'd check (AKA sniff) the armpits of her bodysuits, and if they were particularly pungent, I would soak them with washing-up liquid before putting them in the washing machine.

One day, Rox was standing at the kitchen door, hand over mouth and tears in her eyes.

"Babe," she said, "I feel equal parts horrendous that you have to do this, and also like the luckiest person in the world to have someone so amazing."

Watching me clean her clothes, and realising that I know everything about her and still absolutely adore her, seemed to be incredibly healing. It's absolutely beautiful to share some of our most embarrassing struggles with those we love, and to let them help. To me, it was such an easy task, and I really didn't mind doing it. To her, it meant she wasn't unlovable; in fact, quite the opposite.

We've come a long way since then. Rox is so happy and free, and so much better with personal hygiene. She still does it in her own way, and I imagine a lot of people wouldn't understand, but we don't care about that. We laugh so much about this together. In fact, we even have some common hygiene-related phrases in our house:

Babe, I just got a whiff of BO. I think it's time for a shower.

Babe, you have worn that jumper for seven days straight. Please can I wash it?

Babe, are you going for the wet look here? If not, maybe you could wash your hair?

It's shame free. We find it hilarious. And it works for us.

SUPPORTING AN ADHDer WITH PERSONAL HYGIENE

Your ADHDer isn't failing to meet cleanliness standards. They just have *different* standards. One of the worst things we can do is try and force them into a routine that is utterly draining to them in an effort to make them seem more acceptable to us. They've likely been failing at personal hygiene routines their whole life. So instead, somewhat counterintuitively, we're going to do the opposite. No forced routines, just acceptance, and gentle reminders.

Trust me when I say your ADHDer probably loves feeling clean. But the energy and organisation that takes is not something accessible to them on a daily basis, particularly if they have anything else going on in their life. So our goal is simple: to absolutely love and accept their hygiene habits, to communicate openly with them, and to implement little things that might help ease the burden.

DON'T JUDGE: Don't act shocked, and don't shame your ADHDer. They will be doing enough of that themselves. Get inquisitive about their experience and their historical relationship to personal hygiene. You will most likely find someone who desperately wishes they could be better at these things, but just doesn't know where to start. Due to the amount of shame this topic can carry, being kind and compassionate is paramount.

EXPERIMENT WITH CO-HABITS: Whenever you shower or clean your teeth, check in with your ADHDer. Perhaps they want to do it too. Often having someone there beside them just makes it easier. Again, don't judge and don't use pressure; just let them know what you are up to and invite them to join in. Personal hygiene, like anything, is a skill we develop. And over time, with help and guidance, your ADHDer will start to develop their own habits, from a place of self-esteem as opposed to shame.

USE HUMOUR: At first, this can be a really sensitive topic, so go easy on your ADHDer. Kindness and compassion are the name of the game. But using light-hearted humour can really help to reduce the shame and seriousness of the situation. That might sound like, "I think you could really get the World Record for longest time without a shower!"—always said in a happy, non-judgemental way. Bringing humour to this topic can allow you both to talk about it frankly and honestly.

TRY NOVELTY: We know ADHDers love novelty. If it's new and sparkly, they're in! You can help encourage your ADHDer with basic hygiene tasks like bathing and teeth cleaning by having products you think they will enjoy. For example, ask if they'd like a lavender-oil bath with their favourite scented candle lit, or buy a fancy new electric toothbrush. Try bringing some excitement and joy to this area, as opposed to the crippling shame they will have felt for years. They'll start to love how they feel when they're taking care of themselves, and this will make the habit easier.

SYMPTOM FIVE: STRUGGLES WITH CLEANING THE HOUSE

AKA "Could we please just get a cleaner?"

Picture the scene.

I'm 19 years old.

I'm living away from home for the first time while at university.

Five of my friends and I rent a house in Leamington Spa.

I'm given the nicest room, with a beautiful double bed, while my five mates all had singles.

I have a view over the high street.

A Juliette balcony.

And a fly infestation…

While my friends were experiencing their first taste of adulthood, which is essentially a rather bittersweet thing, what with paying rent and electricity bills and doing our own laundry, I was experiencing my world falling apart.

Why couldn't I keep clean like them?

Why was my room so disgusting?

Why were all my clothes dirty?

There was only one answer: *Because I am useless. A waste of space. Lazy and disgusting.*

When faced with that kind of self-concept, it becomes difficult to see any value in your life, or yourself. Now, fast-forward to the other rite of passage often experienced at university. Not the one where you learn how to do all the boring things required to function in this world, but the one where day drinking is okay and you start steadily working towards a degree in alcoholism. One I passed with flying colours, by the way: I ended up walking into my first AA meeting many years later.

At uni you can drink every day of the week, and no one bats an eye. So, for me, it was the perfect escape. As long as I stayed drunk, I wouldn't have to face the squalid conditions I had created for myself. Plus, being drunk all the time gave me an excuse for being a mess. It was easier to be a piss-head who didn't care about cleaning, than to be a girl who really did care but just had no idea how to do it.

There are a lot of links between ADHD and addiction. I can only speak from my own personal experience, but looking back now, it makes sense that I began to struggle. Alcohol was a daily hit of dopamine: it took the edge off my anxiety; it allowed me to escape from the constant bully inside my own head. I was self-medicating the symptoms of my ADHD and I didn't even know it.

In order to survive the shame of my friends knowing how unclean I was, I wore my messiness like a badge of honour. I'd gloat about not showering for 10 days, and I'd smile proudly as one of my roommates regaled another group of students with the fly infestation story over pints of snakebite on a night out.

Humour and alcohol. That's all I had.

Looking back now, I understand that I simply wasn't equipped to live on my own. My good grades at school had led people to believe I was some kind of genius, and therefore obviously destined to go to university. But nobody once stopped to ask if I had the life skills to live on my own. The gifted child who couldn't clean her own clothes... It was a pretty confusing place to be...

As I watched my five roommates blossom into adulthood, I felt like they had received a manual to life that I never got. It included how and when to wash clothes, make beds, and pay bills. It all seemed so easy for them. This, of course, only made my personal shame worse.

Things continued to deteriorate after I left university. In the years that followed, my friends were holding down jobs, saving up for London houses, meeting lovely ladies who would become their wives, and talking about having children.

Meanwhile, I was living in disgusting spare rooms and basements flats. Wherever I went, whatever new start I gave myself, within weeks it would descend into chaos. I lived out of a suitcase for a decade, because I didn't know how to unpack. Adulthood was a rising tide, and I couldn't swim. I kicked and kicked as the water rose toward my mouth, desperately trying not to drown. How could I be so tired, yet achieving so little? My already rock-bottom self-esteem plummeted even further and took me as close to hell as I have ever been.

I remember one terrible night when I was 29, sat in a basement flat in London, unable to answer the door because of the shame of the mess inside, without the use of my phone or lights because my electricity had been shut off, hands gripping my matted hair... The thought of ending my life felt like a welcome escape. Suicidal ideation called me home, to a place where I didn't have to fail, to live like this, to be such a failure. It could all be over.

Writing this now, I am in tears at how close I came to not being here. At how many layers of shame had been heaped on top of me, to the point where I couldn't carry the weight any more.

Since getting my diagnosis, though, things have changed. I am by no means a domestic goddess, mind you; perhaps the highest title I could hold is domestic jester. However, I make my bed most days, I do the odd load of washing, and I sometimes even remember to hang it up.

In all seriousness, though, a lot of things had to happen for me to attain my domestic jester status.

Getting sober: Stopping the self-medication so I could really feel and face what was happening.

Getting therapy: Beginning to unpack a difficult childhood and some traumatic events I had been through.

Finding a supportive partner: In my case, this meant meeting Rich and learning how to fully love and be loved.

Getting an ADHD diagnosis: Learning to understand myself more fully, and learning to change my internal narrative from one of shame to one of compassion.

This didn't happen overnight, of course. It took me four years. I had so much to unpack, and so much to relearn. Yes, change is absolutely possible. We can grow, be kinder to ourselves, and get better in many areas. But I don't want to sugar-coat things: it takes a lot of time, and a lot of effort.

I also need to point out that I live with Rich. He does the majority of the admin, organisation, and domestic tasks in our house. I am grateful beyond words for his work, and there is no doubt in my mind that were I living alone again, a lot of my struggles would resurface. My support needs are pretty high, and I have the incredible privilege of living with a partner who enjoys assisting in these areas. I know that's not always possible. A lot of you may be single, or in an unsupportive dynamic, or perhaps you are both neurodivergent! I absolutely acknowledge the pain these dynamics can cause, and I am confident that there is still hope for you within these pages.

SUGGESTIONS TO HELP

Stop watching Marie Kondo and Mrs. Hinch. That will never be us. Yes, perhaps there might be a two-week hyperfocus that will have us believing we are domestic gods, but that will come to an end, and we'll crash back down into household hell. We're not good at cleaning. That's fine, though. We're great at loads of other things.

Letting go of the desire for perfection will be our best friend here. Rich and I have decided our house doesn't need to be perfectly clean; it just needs to be okay most of the time. Okay is completely fine. The following are tips that have genuinely helped me become a more functioning member of our household, and I'm grateful to have developed the skills. BUT—remember that your life purpose is not to have a super-tidy house. It's to accept yourself and be happy.

LET GO OF THE SHAME: You are not a disgusting, awful human being. You do not deserve to be bullied by others, or by yourself. No one can hate themselves into a version of themselves that they like. It doesn't work like that. Self-shaming only leads to lower self-belief, and worse conditions. It's time to show kindness and compassion to yourself and learn to understand why you struggle with cleaning.

ASK FOR HELP: I imagine a lot of you nodded when I mentioned feeling like my university friends had received a manual to life that I didn't get. The thing is, we can get access to this manual now, from a safe, loving person in our lives. Ask for help! Ask someone to show you, slowly and clearly, how to use a washing machine, how to clean a mirror without leaving smudges, or how to hang clothes to dry so you don't need to iron them. Take notes, take videos. There is no shame in having some extra tuition when we are struggling.

ONE THING A DAY: When my therapist pushed me to practice cleaning, I was reluctant. "You don't understand, though," I protested. "It's physically impossible for me to do these things." Of course she validated me, agreeing that it *has* been harder for me than most, but she also didn't want me to believe I'd never have these skills. She encouraged me to do one thing a day at home. Whether it was taking a coffee cup downstairs, or hanging up a T-shirt, or pressing start on the dishwasher. Her reasoning was that if you start small, you are more likely to succeed and will slowly start building your self-esteem. And she was right: my one thing a day now has me making the bed with no overwhelm; it's pretty incredible.

PATIENCE: No matter how many cleaning articles you hyperfocus on, you aren't going to turn into Marie Kondo overnight. The trick is to make little improvements on a daily basis that will change your habits and self-beliefs over months and years. Think of the crash dieter who loses a stone in three weeks, only to put it all back on, versus the person who eats a balanced diet and goes to the gym three times per week. Over the long haul, slow and steady wins the race. So go easy on yourself. Don't expect miracles, and celebrate the small stuff.

"What do you mean, 'floordrobe'?!"
Written by Rich

Let me introduce you to *the floordrobe*. A piece of "furniture" used by ADHDers. It's essentially a large carpet space often found in the bedroom that functions not only as a floor, but also as a wardrobe.

I had never seen a floordrobe until Rox moved into my small, pristinely kept two-bed flat in Basingstoke. Suddenly, my immaculately kept carpet (you know the satisfying type of clean where you see the symmetrical Hoover marks?) was covered in band T-shirts, chequered tops with coffee stains, and makeup.

Thank God for the intoxicating chemicals being released when you fall in love because, honestly, without them I don't think I would have made it through Hurricane Rox. At the start of our relationship, I found everything she did absolutely adorable. Makeup on my new carpet? Aww, don't worry. I'll clean it! Ten unworn outfits strewn across the floor I'd just Hoovered? Awww, babe, that is so cute. Let me hang them for you…

So let me take you forward in time. It's pre-ADHD diagnosis, but it's post–being blinded by the honeymoon cocktail. It's late in the evening. It's taken me three hours to get home; the M25 was not playing ball, and I'm in a bad mood.

I pull up to the drive. Thank God I am finally home.

Rox has been cleaning the spare room all day. It's been on the agenda for ages, but today she'd actually taken a day off work to get it done. I do most of the cleaning in the house, which can be a bit frustrating, so having her offer to do this meant a lot.

I open the door and see her sat at the kitchen table. Pots of paint, without lids, scissors, and bits of fabric are everywhere... What the hell is happening?

"Hey, babe..." I say.

She jumps. "Oh, hi, bubby!" she says. I can hear the excitement in her voice. "Look at this!"

She holds up a denim jacket covered in colourful patches, held together with safety pins, with her name painted onto the back. I can't really look at the jacket. My eyes have landed immediately on the red paint splatters on the new wooden table. I feel my frustration start to rise... M25 delay + undiagnosed ADHD wife = not my finest moment.

"Looks great, babe... Please tell me you did the spare room, though?" I'm struggling to hide my annoyance and she can tell.

"Oh my God," she says, horrified. "The spare room! I totally forgot!"

"Babe... You literally took a day off to do it! There is no way you forgot. You obviously just couldn't be bothered. I wish you would just say that instead of making excuses."

She's silent, her bottom lip starting to quiver. She puts her jacket down on the table, her gaze dropping even lower.

Normally I'd jump in to comfort her, but honestly, this behaviour is starting to get to me. I walk heavy-footed up to our bedroom, where I find even more clothes over the floor. My temper boils over. I've genuinely had enough.

Recalling these memories is pretty scary. I can see how easy it would have been for us to feel like we were falling out of love, or were just two very different people. Without the language of ADHD to help us talk about our struggles, we were both left feeling chronically misunderstood.

Rox's diagnosis was a huge turning point for us. We totally changed the way we spoke to each other regarding cleaning. I was able to approach her with curiosity and kindness, as opposed to thinly veiled frustration, which in turn meant she could be a lot more vulnerable with me.

Rather than looking at Rox as someone who was intentionally being lazy and not respecting my time and effort, I was able to see someone who desperately wanted to be part of the household cleaning routine, but simply couldn't. Her pain was very real.

As advised by Rox's therapist, we started small. She worked on doing just one thing a day around the house. Whether she took one cup downstairs, put bleach in one toilet, or hung up her coat, we would celebrate. I'd say thank you, and tell her I was proud of her.

When an ADHD person has felt like a failure in this area their entire life, and been labelled as lazy and selfish, hearing the words *I'm proud of you* is like a magical healing potion. I can see the joy emanating from her every time she gets that validation from me.

Rox's cleaning habits now are so different to when we met. She makes the bed pretty much every day, she always asks to help me with cleaning and laundry, and sometimes I'll come home to a clean kitchen. These are massive victories for her, and it's taken practice, patience and kindness from both of us.

SUPPORTING AN ADHDer WITH CLEANING

If your ADHDer had a choice, they would choose to be good at cleaning. Their space would be immaculate every day. They actually feel calmest and happiest in a clean environment! They don't live in disharmony because they are lazy. They genuinely struggle to be organised and build a semblance of daily routine. Years of failing to be on top of housework will likely have led to a deep sense of personal failure and hopelessness, and it's that we need to tackle, not the cleaning skills themselves.

BE CURIOUS, NOT ANGRY: Don't assume someone is lazy or disrespectful if they aren't good at cleaning. Ask your ADHDer what it feels like to stand in a messy room; ask them if they would know where to start. The likelihood is that it's extremely overwhelming for them, and that this overwhelm has led to avoidance, which in turn has led to not developing what we might call basic skills. Get curious about their story and experience, as opposed to projecting your own standards onto them. Of course, real laziness does exist in this world. And ADHDers are not exempt from it. But look for effort on their behalf. There's a big difference between "I can't make my bed—I have ADHD" and "I find it really difficult to make my bed. I'd really like some help with it, please."

OFFER TO TEACH: I've shown Rox how to fold clothes, how to properly load and start the dishwasher and how to wipe the mirrors without leaving marks. She eagerly learned it all, even taking notes on some occasions, and has worked hard putting it all into practice. Your ADHDer is way more capable than they think they are, and loving, kind, clear instructions can be an absolute game changer. As Rox wrote earlier, they likely feel like they missed out on reading the life manual that everybody else got. Share that knowledge with them.

CELEBRATE THE WINS: It can feel strange to say "well done" to someone for bringing a coffee mug downstairs after you cleaned the entire house at the weekend. It's difficult to reconcile those two things. However, an ADHDer whose progress is noted and celebrated is going to build self-esteem and skills a lot more quickly than someone whose efforts are ignored. Realise that by celebrating and thanking your ADHDer for their contributions, you are helping turn around a lifelong narrative of ineptness.

DON'T MOCK THEM: It would be really easy to make fun of someone for not being able to do things you can do in your sleep. But please remember, your ADHDer will likely feel a lot of embarrassment and shame around their difficulties with these basic tasks. Be inquisitive and supportive, but don't mock, bully or shame.

SYMPTOM SIX: FINANCIAL ISSUES

AKA "Oh, I didn't look at the price…"
Written by Rox

There was a loud knock on the door of my basement flat. Obviously I didn't answer; ADHDers don't really like opening doors. This brings with it the anxiety of not knowing who is on the other side, and which human mask you will have to put on. Plus, who knocks on a door uninvited?! Psychopaths, that's who. So I did what any ADHD 29-year-old would do: I ran into my bedroom and hid under the bed.

The knocking continued, now with the addition of a scary male voice.

"Miss Emery… are you in there?" *BANG, BANG, BANG.*

My heart was beating out of my chest, sweat dripping down my forehead. *Who the hell is this at my door? Why does he know my name?* I was convinced he was going to break in. I held my breath. *Please, God, just go away. I'll start going to church. Seriously, God, whatever you want. Just help me.*

The banging stopped for a moment. I heard more footsteps outside. Was he leaving? No. The steps were getting louder. Now someone else was coming down to my door. *Jesus Christ*, I thought. *There's more than one of them!*

Then came the sound of heavy machinery. A chainsaw, I think. *Am*

I in a horror film? Is this where I actually die? I hear the sound of cutting and crashing metal as hammers hit against the outside wall of my flat. *Are they breaking down the wall?*

Seconds felt like hours. When the men finally left, I started crying. I had genuinely been fearing for my life. When I was certain they had left I crawled out from under the bed, my anxiety still higher than Snoop Dogg. I walked cautiously towards my front door, in case they were hiding outside and tricking me into a false sense of security. I peeked outside. No men, but a hell of a lot of mess.

I picked up the brown envelope that had come through the letter box.

NOTICE: EDF ENERGY

It all began clicking into place… *Ah—my unpaid energy bills.*

I opened my front door, slightly soothed by the official documentation that this was more of a bailiff situation than outright murder.

There, in all its glory, was my new electricity box. The pay-as-you-go type. I'd lost access to a normal meter due to so many unpaid bills and unanswered letters.

How am I going to tell my landlord? The shame hit me like a tidal wave.

Not only did I now have the excruciating task of explaining to my lovely landlord the absolute mess that had been made by his front door, I also had to figure out how to top up the meter—and remember to do it regularly.

I'm ashamed to tell you I didn't do either of these things. It wasn't until I was evicted the following year for not paying rent that the landlord found out the old meter had been replaced. And as for using the new pay-as-you-go meter, I found myself regularly sat in total darkness with no power and no Wi-Fi. Some days this was due to lack of funds; other days it was due to not having the energy to go to the corner shop to buy a top-up. The irony of these being some of my *darkest* days is not lost on me.

I've used an extreme example of my difficulties with financial organisation to highlight how bad things can be: undiagnosed ADHD can take a person to the very edge of their tolerance.

And of course, this incident, although it was certainly one of my more memorable financial meltdown moments, was not the only one. I have lived a life coloured by overdrafts, maxed-out credit cards, unpaid bills, CCJs (county court judgements for debt), a bad credit rating, and the overwhelming shame of not being able to organise my finances.

One of the first things that really helped me start to sort out my money mess was getting sober, something I did in 2018. Drunk me was an incredibly reckless spender.

"Shots for everyone!" I'd yell at my local dive bar, knowing full well the cost would mean I couldn't top up my electricity meter for the next week.

The combination of alcohol and undiagnosed ADHD equals financial ruin. After getting sober, though, I couldn't run from these problems anymore.

The truth is, I had never opened a letter from HMRC (the British tax authority), my phone bill, a notice from an energy company, a council tax notification, or a bill from my credit card companies.

I'd essentially been running away from debt my whole life, changing addresses in the hope I wouldn't be found. And somehow managing to make enough money to make it through month by month.

Stopping alcohol wasn't a magic solution. It did take the craziest expenses off the table, though: no champagne ordered in clubs, no drugs, no late-night binges. But I still couldn't get a grip on finances. Even sober, I still found myself overspending, and running up credit card debt.

My solution? Bury my head in the sand. Only, it's harder to do that sober. Without eight Desperados to take the edge off, my sheer lack of organisation and my sinking financial status were staring me in the face. Yet again I found myself buried beneath a mountain of shame.

I ended up living in a friend's spare room, unable to pay the £350 they had suggested as rent. I was 34. Let me remind you of my "gifted child" status growing up; there was simply nothing more humiliating than being in this position. Again, the only conclusion I could draw was that I was an absolutely dreadful human being who deserved all of this.

And then, by some miracle from the gods I don't believe in, I met Rich. We fell in love so spectacularly. I felt like I had finally found a home, something I had been searching for since the death of my mother, a decade earlier. Rich's job? A bank manager. *"Is this man an actual angel?"* I said to myself.

I was really honest with him about my financial difficulties. It was the first time I'd really let anyone see how much debt I was in, or talked about my struggles to control my spending. He was never fazed. I truly expected him to walk away, but he never did. He helped me open my letters, write emails, and cut up some credit cards. He also reflected back to me kindly when I was being reckless.

When we met, my credit rating was very poor. It's now excellent. I'm still gobsmacked by that… *Me?! An excellent credit rating?!* It's one of my proudest achievements.

I'm still not great with money, however. I love expensive things, and I'm very impulsive. But I accept help. I take feedback. I try really hard. And God apparently loves a trier. I don't have credit cards. I don't have access to my savings. And I check in with Rich before big impulsive spends. We have a joint account for bills that I pay into. We live in a house where the electricity bill gets paid, and no one's banging down the door. For that, I am forever grateful.

SUGGESTIONS TO HELP

Credit card debt, payday loans, unopened red letters, final demands, and bailiffs. The reality of being in debt, and having ADHD, is so incredibly frightening. It can feel like you are drowning with no way out, coupled with blaming yourself for getting into the mess in the first place. If you are in debt, please ask for help. It is imperative you remove the constant state of stress you are living in, as it is extremely damaging to your mental health.

Once you're out of crippling debt, it's about staying that way. That will take sacrifices on your part, and making choices that may feel uncomfortable. For example, not having credit cards. Overspending will always be a risk factor, so we need to protect ourselves as much as we can to ensure we don't destabilise our lives.

ASK FOR HELP: It can be utterly overwhelming to be in debt with a pile of unopened bills. As well as being devastating for your mental health. Opening the first letter can feel like climbing Mount Everest. Ask someone you trust to sit down with you and help you, whether that's a parent, partner, friend, or therapist. It's a game changer to have some moral support facing up to something that feels so scary. There is nothing to be ashamed about. Asking for help might sound like this: "I have ADHD and I really struggle to stay organised financially. I've let things go too far, and it feels impossible to me. Would you sit with me while I open these letters please? I'm really scared."

OPEN THE LETTERS: Stacks of unopened bills are far worse than whatever is hiding inside them. If you open just one of them today, you have done something amazing. There's often an email address on the letter when people are chasing money, so you won't need to ring anyone. You can email them with an apology and ask if they would consider a repayment plan.

CREDIT CARDS: Honestly, my advice would be not to have them, unless you absolutely need them for basic living expenses. Giving up your credit cards is the safest way to ensure you aren't maxing them out time and time again. ADHDers suffer with impulse control; it's just safer not to have these things on hand. If you do have to have one, set up a direct debit from your bank to make sure you never miss a payment: missed payments can negatively affect your credit rating.

PRACTISE: You aren't awful or stupid. You have just been practising overspending and avoiding the horrible consequences. It's time to start practising other skills—very slowly and, ideally, with help. Practise saving a little each month. Practise opening a brown envelope. Practise filling the little online shopping cart and not pressing BUY. These are skills that take some learning. You will get better—I promise. You are fighting against years of evidence that has told you that you are terrible with money. It will take some time to change that internal dialogue. But it's so important that you do. As we've mentioned a lot in this book, shame does not lead to changed behaviour. You must start with kindness and acceptance before trying to change.

"Why has £1000 just come out of the joint account?"
Written by Rich

I have worked in a bank since I was 16 years old, beginning as a cashier and moving through the ranks to become manager of one of the UK's biggest branches. I'm very good with money; my credit rating has been consistently 999 for as long as I can remember…

Working in a bank, though, I have seen some heartbreaking situations—customers struggling to make ends meet and coming to us for help. I have boundless compassion for people who find themselves in a financial hole.

I haven't always been well off. I became a dad as a teenager, and the sole provider for a household of four. I had to cycle two hours to and from work, often in the rain, and make a £40 weekly shopping budget work. I vividly remember walking around Lidl with a pen and paper, costing things to the penny, and often having to put items back.

I cannot for the life of me imagine what someone in my position would do if they also had ADHD. My younger years were a really tough time for me, and I am so grateful that my brain finds organisation and numbers simple. I relied on those skills to get me through some very trying times.

Over the years, as my career progressed, I started to earn more money and became comfortable. But the Lidl mindset? It has never left me. I am always price conscious, I err on the side of caution, and I cannot fathom people who would spend more than £30 on a pair of trainers. Enter Rox…

When we met, she was struggling to pay £350 a month in rent for the spare room she was living in, yet within weeks of us starting to date she had bought photo frames, candles and plants for my flat. Here was someone who had next to nothing, was up to her eyeballs in debt, yet was choosing to buy me gifts because she just couldn't think of me living in such an empty and un-homely space…

Of course, generosity like that can be such a beautiful trait. But it's also one that can cause trouble for Rox. She will always be the first to buy people things, things she can't actually afford. As we got closer, Rox opened up to me about her financial struggles, and I was stunned at the amount of stress she was secretly living with.

Her biggest fear was that her credit card debt and bank loans would affect any future mortgage that we wanted to get together. She wept as she told me how she hadn't opened mail for years, of the anxiety she felt around money, and how she felt useless as a human being because of this.

To her, these financial struggles were a monstrous, shameful secret that she had to hide in order to be loved. To me, it was a problem with a simple solution. I entered bank manager mode.

There was absolutely nothing about her situation that couldn't be sorted out. So I helped her do just that. We began paying off debts, she gave up her credit cards, we worked on her credit rating, and after a couple of years, she was debt free.

We now live in a lovely house that we rent together (in spite of her having a CCJ), and we are saving up to buy a house in the future. Despite the crippling levels of anxiety and stress Rox's financial struggles brought her, she still gravitates towards spending a lot of money—the most expensive hotels, makeup, holidays, and gifts. The difference is that now she will chat to me first. She allows me to be part of the process, which has helped massively with impulse purchases.

That part of her that wants to rack up massive credit card bills? It's still there. Only now she is more supported. Rox hasn't changed—and that might sound crazy to some people, but her brain just doesn't work like mine. The CCJs, the shame, the anxiety—none of these are enough to change her brain wiring. She's always searching for that hit of happiness that impulsive spending brings her. I understand that now, and I will never shame her for it.

Rox has been reminded over and over again by me that she is not in trouble—it's something that comes up a lot. We've both learned to be really patient and kind to each other, to try and understand the other person's perspective. Honestly? We've rubbed off on each other. Yes, I have helped Rox not spend herself into a hole, but occasionally when we have the money, Rox has encouraged us to do something lovely, or have a weekend away, something I struggle with due to my past. We balance each other out, and as a result, we live a beautiful, stable life together.

SUPPORTING AN ADHDer STRUGGLING WITH FINANCES

ADHD spending is compulsive. It often leaves your ADHDer feeling guilty over their choices, not to mention living with the consequences of spending money they don't have. Of course, your ADHDer is in charge of their choices, and we absolutely do not want to control them. However, if they are struggling and they ask for help, we can be a lifeline here. Opening letters, talking them through things, letting them know it will be okay—all these things can go such a long way to lighten the load they have been carrying.

Reflecting back reality to them in a kind way can help your ADHDer start to grow their understanding of money. They may have been using spending as a way to feel better momentarily, as opposed to thought-out budgeting. As always, kindness and compassion lead the way when we want to help.

ASK AND LISTEN: Ask your ADHDer what their relationship with money is like, and whether they have any struggles. Don't shame or blame them; just let them know it's not as bad as they think it is. Also assure them that there are a few simple things you can do as a team to remedy any situation, whether that's opening a pile of letters together or helping the person to set up a payment plan.

CREDIT CARDS: If your ADHDer has credit cards, offer to look after them. Sometimes just removing the temptation of a £500 shopping spree is enough to help them get control of their financial situation. To be very clear, this is *not* about controlling your ADHDer's money. Rather, it's an offer to support them—but only if they're open to it.

CELEBRATE WINS: If your ADHDer choses something that's on sale, a medium-priced hotel, or last season's trainers, acknowledge the behaviour. It's difficult for them not to act on impulse and follow the dopamine hit of the biggest spends. Every time they do make a sensible decision, it's worth noticing and validating.

HELP THEM BUDGET: Help your ADHDer work out how much their bills are every month. Then, help them set up regular payments, from a separate account, each time they get paid to cover all the bills. After expenses are taken care of, all the money they have left is theirs to play with and the damage they can do is limited! They have likely never been shown how budgeting and credit scoring work, so patience and understanding are key.

SYMPTOM SEVEN: TASK AVOIDANCE

AKA "I will literally do anything other than what I am supposed to be doing…"
Written by Rox

In my third term of my first year at university, I was struggling to prepare for my end-of-year exams. I'd managed to clock up a dismal 5 percent attendance at the lectures, opting instead for nights out, hangovers, and downloading rock music from LimeWire.

With the pressure of my final exams looming, and some illegally bought amphetamines from the internet, I was ready to pull a few all-nighters and get the work done. Working under extreme pressure was the only way I could actually accomplish anything.

So there I was, happily on my way to visit the library for the very first time (despite having been on campus for over nine months), a spring in my step, ready to take on the mammoth task in front of me: to cram a year's work into a couple of nights.

I was feeling confident and a little wired, perhaps both symptoms of the internet-bought amphetamines. I walked down the two flights of stairs in my halls and was about to leave when I saw some of my close friends sitting in the common room. I popped my head round the door.

"Yo, guys! What's up?"

They looked up, a little surprised to see me not holding a drink.

"Ughh," one of them groaned. "It's supply-and-demand laws, that's what's up. Just can't get my head around it."

It so happened that this very diligent friend, who had in fact managed near perfect attendance all year, was struggling with a particular economics concept. I felt that fiery focus ignite in me and a desire to help them with this module. After all, I'd studied economics at A level and somehow managed to blag an A, so this stuff must come easily to me, right?

"Give me an hour!" I shouted. I ran back upstairs, loaded up my thick, brick-like early 2000s laptop and began refreshing my memory on the economic principles of supply and demand. Ah, yes… It all came flooding back. My brain was firing on all cylinders: graphs, charts, supply and demand curves. I could see these ideas so clearly. My own revision plans were out of the window. I was now an economics teacher with a very important job to do.

After a decent refresher, I went back downstairs and told everyone to grab a drink: it was economics lesson time. Then, standing tall, arms waving like a frantic professor (or an 18-year-old on amphetamines), I began explaining the economic principles they were struggling to grasp in crystal-clear, impassioned, and absolutely-impossible-to-ignore terms.

After 20 minutes, heads started nodding; light bulbs were going off. I could see it was clicking, and I was absolutely joyful. Another hour rolled by and the 99p beers we had been drinking started kicking in. A little fuzzy-headed from both the super-speed I'd ingested and the complex economic principles I was vomiting out at my "students," I decided not to go to the library.

So there I was, pushing back my own studies, on which I was already chronically behind, for the dopamine high of giving somebody else an economics lesson. I didn't even like economics…

This is a classic example of ADHD task avoidance, and it has dominated my life. It doesn't matter what I am *supposed* to be doing; my brain will feverishly look for something—anything—else to do and make that thing so incredibly desirable, I've got no choice but to jump down the rabbit hole of that new task.

It's not simply about avoiding certain tasks like cleaning, administration or studying. It's about avoiding *whatever* it is that is *most important at that time*. Take cleaning, for example, something I struggle to find the motivation for every day. But tell me I need to respond to an urgent work email? My brain will fire up till I'm conducting a Mrs Hinch–style clean of our house! I will do anything but reply to that email.

If I'm meant to be ringing HSBC to order a new bank card? Well, this suddenly feels like a great time to organise the bits-and-bobs drawer I've been meaning to tackle for two years.

Meant to be sending out wedding invitations? Actually, this feels like the perfect time for a new set of self-applied gel nails.

My level of task avoidance is such that I become physically obsessed by the thing I am *not* meant to be doing. I just have to do that thing right away. Which, unfortunately, means the really important thing I was meant to be doing does not get attended too.

Okay. So now you understand the extent of my task avoidance. With that in mind, please imagine me being employed.

Yeah... I wouldn't hire me, either.

I've had many jobs in my life, many of which haven't gone well. I imagine you aren't too surprised to hear that. Employers over the years have been impressed by my obvious passion and creative ideas, but frustrated at my lack of ability to see things through. I've been an underachiever forever, feeling like something great was just out of reach.

That is, until I found my current job, in an area I fondly refer to as my forever fixation. And that's songwriting. Starting to work as a full-time songwriter happened around the time I got sober and my journey towards therapy and diagnosis began. It's no surprise that this job has been the most successful one I've had. I write with different people every day, and I start a new song every day. There's a creative challenge to work towards as a team, and a beautiful pay-out when we leave with a playable demo at the end of the day. I honestly cannot think of a job more suited to my brain.

Again, though, working at a job you love isn't a magic cure-all for task avoidance. There are plenty of administrative aspects to songwriting that I fall behind on. Need the lyrics sent for that song we did six months ago? Sorry, mate—not a chance. The lucky thing is, the most important aspect of my job is the song itself, and I have other people to help pick up my administrational slack.

At home, too, I try really hard to do what I am meant to be doing. I don't want Rich to have to do all the housework and admin alone. That isn't fair. I push myself to be better, and when I notice task avoidance kicking in, I will call it out, put on a Queen playlist, and re-focus myself. I have to have strategies to get things done, and it's going to look a little different to most people, but… I now have more control over my actions. Which ultimately is a good thing.

SUGGESTIONS TO HELP

At the very core of ADHD is an issue with attention. So, hey, it's no surprise our minds are often drifting off task. This isn't about forcing you to stay on track, or trying to fundamentally change the way you are wired. It's about learning to work with your task avoidance.

It isn't a moral failing to get off task. Your mind is just a wandering hippie in a world full of sergeant majors. And that's okay. Recognising this symptom, and understanding how to treat it with kindness, will allow you to feel more positively about yourself, which will in turn help you complete important tasks from a place of self-belief rather than self-hatred.

RECOGNISE IT: If you are meant to be cleaning your room and you find yourself sat cross-legged on the floor reading every birthday card you've ever been sent, call it out. *I am seriously distracted right now. I'm going to get back to the task at hand and come back to these cards later.* Every time you are able to do this, you build a habit of getting to choose where your focus goes.

DO THE IMPORTANT TASK FIRST: If you have something to do today, do it now. I mean *right now.* Put this book down and go and do it. Because we only have right now, or never. Go make yourself a coffee, and do that one thing you're putting off till later. The longer the day goes on, the more likely you are to see something on your phone, hear something in conversation or trip over something you've left on the floor that has the potential to derail your whole day.

TELL PEOPLE: Let your friends, family and colleagues know that you have ADHD and are incredibly easily distracted. If you feel comfortable, give them permission to call you out in a calm and kind way. I can't tell you the number of times Rich has simply said "I thought you were finishing that song," or something similar, and it has bought me back into reality. Every time, with a laugh, I realise the ADHD avoidance monster has struck again.

SEE THE POSITIVES: If you're meant to clean your bedroom, and you end up avoiding it by doing something totally random, you gain absolutely nothing from that other than delaying the original task and feeling like you've let yourself down. However, if you're on a walk and meant to be taking it all in, and then your brain suddenly jumps to a business idea, well, that's a definite upside! I've written ideas that went on to be platinum-selling records while in the back of an Uber. In fact, our ADHD_Love TikTok was started after Rich told me it was time to go to sleep, and because I wanted to avoid that, we had to start it that very evening!

"So... cleaning is easy only if you're avoiding calling the bank? Got it."
Written by Rich

Here's how I approach doing a task, written as an equation:

(Say I will do X) + (I actually do X) = everything is great

(Say I will do X) + (I don't do X) = everything is not great

Words and actions have always been linked for me. If I say I'm going to clean the house, it's getting done. On the very rare occasion I say I am going to do something and then don't, I don't feel great. It feels to me like something is slipping away, like I'm getting a bit behind on life. I'm not sure whether you could call it anxiety, but it's definitely a little uncomfortable.

I like to avoid not feeling great, so 99 percent of the time I tend to just do the thing, whether it's laundry, house cleaning, or the weekly shop. It's all very organised in my mind. I genuinely thought most people operated in this way, and if they didn't, I saw them as lazy or otherwise "not good."

Then I met Rox. Her task equation looks a little like this:

(Says she will do X) + (forgets to do X) + (thinks of something else to do instead) = very happy until she remembers about X again, in which case she will have crippling anxiety.

This way of working makes zero sense to me, and mine made no sense to her, and in the beginning of our relationship we used to annoy each other quite a bit.

Here's a list of phrases that DO NOT WORK at all if you're trying to get someone back on task.

- *Just do it! I don't understand why you are delaying.*
- *Stop painting that jacket! You are wasting time.*
- *You know you are gonna have anxiety avoiding this. What are you doing?*
- *You'll feel better if you just get it done. Come on.*
- *Shall I just do it for you?*

Without me realising it, all these tactics were my attempts to change how Rox processes tasks. I was trying to project onto her what works for me, as opposed to working with her brain and what works for her. That can—and did—feel a lot like judgement, shame, and being misunderstood.

The more I rolled my eyes at her, the more she delayed a task. The more I told her to just do it, the more likely she was to go and start crafting in the other room. You see, my brain is a military sergeant, and Rox's is a meandering hippie.

And that meandering hippie doesn't just wander off to find something to do instead of stacking the dishwasher; they can also wander off mid-conversation. I cannot tell you the number of times we've been chatting, and then I see her eyes glaze over and go slightly crossed, a sure-fire sign she's zoned out.

In the beginning, her zoning out could be upsetting for me, especially if I was sharing something important. It was awkward for us both when she realised she'd drifted off to her spaceship. Each time, not wanting to be rude, she forced herself back into the conversation. Whatever she was thinking became, to her, some shameful secret that couldn't be shared. And I was often left feeling like she didn't care what I had to say. It's very easy to take someone's ADHD behaviours personally, especially if you don't know that's what you're dealing with!

Since her diagnosis, however, things have absolutely changed. I never take her zone-outs as a personal attack. Instead, I just call them out in the moment, often with humour. She is always apologetic. She'll share with me the weird and wonderful place she drifted off to, and then she's right back in the room with me. She doesn't have to feel ashamed, or hide the fact that she's drifted off. And now, I find I love that part of her as much as the present part.

In answer to "Babe, what are you thinking?" I get some pretty awesome responses:

"I was just writing a Christmas song in my head."

"I was trying to figure out if I can make rainbow resin."

"I was thinking how many minutes I need to run in the gym to get curry tonight."

What's not to love?!

That being said, in life, and in love, it's important to be able to focus on a specific task, whether it's having a significant conversation, cleaning an apartment before moving out, or collecting information for a tax return: humans have to be able to complete tasks. So, although I know the wandering hippie of Rox's mind will always take the scenic route, I'm always there with a map back home, via the path that needs to be walked. Rox needs a little extra help getting things done, gentle reminders to get back on task, and friendly call-outs when she wanders off.

SUPPORTING AN ADHDer WITH TASK AVOIDANCE

Your ADHDer's brain is a wandering hippie. Screaming at them to get back on track will only send them further *off* track. It can be frustrating to watch someone complete tasks in what feels like a totally nonsensical way to you, but this is where we need to remember how very different brains can be.

The average school and first-job experiences for most ADHDers consist of being screamed at for just existing and of being shamed for their lack of structured focus. The most healing thing we can do is allow them to wander off. No shouting, no shaming. If something really needs to be done on a deadline, you discuss it calmly, from a place of love.

GENTLY CALL IT OUT: If your ADHDer zones out mid-conversation, or if they are meant to be doing task X and you see them manically going towards task Y, just say kindly, "Looks like you're a bit distracted right now. What's going on for you?" Allowing them a safe space to share the many mysteries and voyages of their brains only helps bring you closer, and then back to the task at hand.

DON'T INTERRUPT: If your ADHDer is working on a task they're actually meant to be doing, don't ask questions about anything else. Other input could very easily knock them off course and send them in a new, unfocused direction. We want to make the most of the times when hyperfocus kicks in exactly when it's meant to!

SET A TIME LIMIT: If your ADHDer simply cannot get back to the task at hand because they *have* to do this other thing, then setting a time limit for them can be really helpful. Whether it's five minutes to read through all the birthday cards they've ever been sent, or ten minutes to research which parts of *The Blindside* film are actually true, having boundaries around how long they can wander off task is really helpful.

BE INQUISITIVE: Just because your ADHDer seems to be avoiding a task, that doesn't mean that wherever their brains are taking them instead is of no value. On the one hand, if they were meant to be cleaning the room and instead they're downstairs going through a bits-and-bobs drawer, there's not much to inquire about. But if their mind has wandered off to investigate a creative or ingenious idea, listen to it. Some of the world's most famous creators and inventors have had ADHD, so don't forget that some deviations from task can in fact lead to life-changing ideas.

SYMPTOM EIGHT: STRUGGLES WITH OBJECT CONSTANCY

AKA "OMG, I am so sorry! I thought I replied to this!"
Written by Rox

I grew up in an era before we had mobile phones. That's going to tell you a lot about my age. Please remember, every story has two sides, and the twice-yearly Botox I get in a clinic on Harley Street is the other side of that particular story...

In a world without mobile phones, friendships were formed face-to-face:

- Talking in the back of maths class
- Kissing boys and girls round the back of the local youth club
- Trying to buy booze underage from your local shop
- Getting blackout drunk on vodka and passing out in a park

That's the basis of true and authentic friendship right there... Ever said you were sleeping around at a friend's house, while your friend said the same thing to their parents, and then spent the night drinking cider together on a park bench? True connection.

Of course, sometimes we would use the archaic home phone to keep in touch, but most of the time, friends were the people we actually saw every day. I had a very close group of friends throughout secondary school and college, but when 18 came around, we all went our own separate ways. A little like the best Ed Sheeran song ever to be written…

A few stayed in our hometown and had kids early.

Some got married (and divorced).

One did an apprenticeship and started a business.

A couple went to the local uni.

A couple went further afield to university.

Some moved countries in search of pastures new.

One didn't make it past 19…

I went to university. With two teacher parents and that gifted kid thing hanging over me, I didn't have much of a choice. I'd been accepted into Warwick, which I was assured was *one of the best universities in the country.* So, in the month of my nineteenth birthday, my parents and I packed all my things into the boot of my dad's car, and he drove me three hours to my first home away from home: the university halls where I would spend the next three years of my life, drinking, having sex, and missing lectures… Quite the education.

What I never expected was how difficult it would be to maintain those "We'll be best friends forever" friendships back at home. The people I grew up with, whom I loved dearly and who knew me the most, sort of ceased to exist for me. You see, I'm so utterly and heavily invested in what is right in front of me that everything else fades into distant memory. My attention is like a flashlight: it's a very bright, focused beam, and when it's shining on something I see that thing illuminated in every detail. But it can only focus on one small thing at a time. It cannot light the whole sky. So those things outside the beam? They fade into the blackness.

I tried to stay in touch when the pangs of loneliness and nostalgia hit—the odd Facebook message here, the promise to meet up at the local pub at Christmas there—but it just wasn't enough. My friendship group back home were growing closer and keeping in touch despite the distance, and I was drifting away. My growing feelings of sadness and shame became too much to handle, so of course, I drank to forget, giving myself fully to my new university life.

My contact with my old friends became fraught with apologies and explanations. I didn't want them to think I didn't care, but I had no language to explain what was happening; all I had was my behaviour, which, to them, looked like the actions of someone who had moved on and forgotten about her closest friends.

I'm so sorry—I've only just seen this, yet another Facebook DM would read. I must have sent that same apology twenty times. Eventually the shame of my failures to communicate became too much, so I stopped trying. "If they're going to think I'm awful, and rude, well… I may as well be that way," was my reasoning. Oh, if I could only go back and tell them how much I loved and valued them, but how much I struggled with digital communication, then maybe I would have more than one childhood friend now in my thirties.

(Nicki, if you're reading this: I don't deserve you, and your dedication to keeping our friendship alive has changed my life in ways you will never know. Thank you. You are beautiful and kind, and I am so lucky to call you a best friend.)

I was 24 when I missed the first wedding, simply because I didn't open, or subsequently reply to the invite. I remember the sheer shame of opening Facebook to discover that it was the day of my old best friend's wedding. And I wasn't there. I sent an apology, trying desperately to express my disgust in myself for missing all the lead-up and the wedding itself, and for the amount of pain I must have caused her. Of course, it was too little, too late, and rightly so. That was her day. She did not deserve my pity party, or my excuses for why I wasn't there.

Those days spelled the end of a number of my high school friendships. As I mentioned, we were a very close group, so missing a wedding is kind of a cardinal sin. Losing my childhood friends hurt like hell, and I had no one to blame but myself. My self-concept as an awful, selfish human being only deepened. I believed to my core that I was not deserving of friends, and that I would lose every connection that I ever made. That became a self-fulfilling prophecy.

As I got further into my 20s, and apps like WhatsApp became more widespread, my struggles only intensified. Of course, these were made worse by the sheer volume of alcohol I was drinking on a daily basis just to try and make it through each day. Drinking was a way to soothe the pain of my failures. I could forget all the lost friends, the broken relationships, the unachieved potential… Just three drinks in and my anxiety was calmed, and I'd be fully present in whatever self-destruction was on the menu for that night. Until, of course, I woke up, hung over, in squalid conditions, feeling even worse… and so the cycle would begin again.

When I first heard the term "object constancy" and how ADHDers struggle with this, I wept like a baby. These two simple words meant I wasn't the worst human to ever live, but instead that I had ADHD and struggled with remembering things that weren't right in front of me.

This is the phenomenon of "out of sight, out of mind." If you're not physically in front of me, it's incredibly difficult to keep you in mind. When we are together, it can be the most connected, hilarious, and intimate of moments, but the second we are not? I can't recall those feelings, or our connection. I forget you exist unless I am looking at you. This sounds pretty selfish, doesn't it? And I suppose it is. I have wanted desperately to change this part of myself. It's caused sleepless nights and guilt so strong it's made me hurt myself. I don't want anyone else to suffer in that way.

Since my ADHD diagnosis, I haven't become better at keeping in touch with people on the phone. But I've gained the confidence to let people know that I struggle with communication. That often looks something like this:

"Hey! I really struggle with keeping up to date with texts. I'd love to go for a coffee and a face-to-face chat. Can we get a date in?"

I'm honest because I don't feel shame any more. It's okay that I struggle with text messages. I've got loads of other awesome skills, and catching up in person is way better anyway! People always receive this sort of request well, and in fact, lots of my friends have similar brains, as it turns out, and we get to laugh about it together. Often messages come with a "Feel free to reply in 2026" disclaimer so no one feels any "textpectations"!

Society says that you have to be in touch and available all the time in order to show that you care about someone. That's not how it works for me. Occasionally a video call or text will be fun, but I much prefer meeting face-to-face. Since my diagnosis, I've contacted some of the friends who had slipped out of my life due to unanswered texts, sincerely apologised for my behaviour and offered a commitment to do better. This wasn't an over-promise to come back to every text on time, mind you. I've done that before—setting myself up to fail, to disappoint someone yet again. This time, it was a genuine desire to connect with them in ways that I was able to actually follow through on. Every single friend that I've approached, some even after years, has welcomed me back with open arms and has been incredibly understanding of the way things have been. I couldn't be more grateful for that.

SUGGESTIONS TO HELP

Calendar reminders to text friends, promises to do better with communication, and yet another apology… It's time to break the cycle. We struggle with constant, structured communication, and that is okay. The following tips won't tell you how to meet all the weird communication expectations of this world. Instead, they will help you to share your inner world with those you love, to let them know that communication can be a struggle, and to find ways to make your relationship work. Being honest about who you are will truly deepen any relationship, more than timely text message replies could ever do.

KNOW THAT IT'S OKAY: I want you to know something deeply in your core: you do not have to be good at replying to text messages in order to be loved. You are not an awful person because you forget to reply to people, whoever they may be. It's okay not to use texting as your preferred medium for friendship.

BE HONEST: We don't have to be good at texting to deserve friendship, but we do have to be honest. Due to societal norms around communication, when we don't reply, it can feel like rejection to the other person, and we don't want that. Share with your friends and family that you find frequent communication on the phone really difficult, that it's got nothing to do with how much you care about them, and ask to work together on a plan that's satisfying for both of you. For example, you might try a video call at a scheduled time or meeting up face-to-face.

STOP THE SHAME SPIRAL: One late reply to one text message is not a big deal. But if you leave it two weeks, then your friend checks in again, and then because of the shame you are feeling you ignore that one too, well, you are digging a big anxious hole for yourself! If you are in that situation right now, it's time to end the shame spiral. Take a deep breath, and send a text or voice note. Just say something like this: "I'm so sorry. I've been finding communicating on the phone really tough. I'm sorry if that's made you feel uncared for or ignored. It's something I struggle with. I'd love to catch up in person, though, if you are open to it?" A friend is going to meet you with non-judgement and compassion.

DON'T READ A MESSAGE IF YOU CAN'T REPLY: This is by no means a cure-all, and I often mess up by reading a message and then forgetting to text back. The unlucky person might be Rich, my dad, or one of my best friends. However, this one little trick, coupled with sharing that I struggle with communication, has helped. **Don't read a message if you're not going to reply to it**. Don't open the text or WhatsApp unless you're in the headspace to answer the message. The notification will stay there as a little reminder for when you later forget, and for me, there is something less anxiety-inducing about an unread text than suddenly recalling one I've read and not gone back to.

"It's been eight hours since I've heard from you. Everything okay?"
Written by Rich

Hi, bubby. Just to let you know I love you! What time are you home so I can cook dinner? xx

READ

It's been four hours…

Is she okay?

Has she hurt herself?

Has she fallen out of love with me?

Has she met someone else?

I'm aware I'm catastrophising here… but why isn't she texting back? Even if something really bad hasn't happened, I still need to know when she's back for dinner. This just feels rude.

What you're reading was a pretty regular occurrence for me before Rox's diagnosis. After the initial honeymoon phase of our relationship had worn off, I suppose in a way I was Rox's hyperfocus for a while. Her texting habits totally changed. We went from being in contact 24/7 to hours going by before she would reply. This would often happen when she was at work, and it sent my anxiety through the roof…

Keeping in touch with people I care about comes naturally to me and always has. Whether that's catching up with my brother on WhatsApp, playing video games with my dad who lives in Spain, or checking in with my kids when they are not with me, it's just not something I need to try hard at.

Rox leaving me on "read" for a few hours, though, triggered some of my own anxieties. I was really honest with her about what I projected onto the silence, and she was always very apologetic, promising to do better. I could tell she was distressed by how much she was upsetting me, and for a few days her behaviour would improve. But… it would always slip back to being inconsistent.

The *only* story that made sense to me was that, deep down, she just didn't care about me. After all, sending a text to someone you love, when they've told you it's important to them, is extremely easy, right?

Without Rox's diagnosis, I'm not sure we would have got through our differing communication habits. It was only after her diagnosis that I was able to realise this wasn't anything to do with me. It wasn't personal. It was a symptom of a neurodivergent brain. So I flipped the script: I took back the power to control my own emotions, to not project my insecurity into the five-hour waits for a reply, and just opt for a stance of trust and belief.

I've now removed all expectation from Rox to reply, told her it's absolutely okay if she forgets, that I'll be okay, and just to call or text if there is something important I need to know. I have never in my life seen relief like I saw in Rox after that. I saw her shoulders actually drop, after thirty years of trying to get on top of something her brain wasn't built for.

I don't expect texts from her when she goes to work, or when she is busy focusing on something else. I know that when she gets home, I'll have her full attention, and I can hear about her day, and vice versa. We have worked hard to remove the shame and pressure she felt from struggling with digital communication, and I have learned to love and be grateful for all the other ways she expresses her love for me. The funny thing is, since talking openly about all this and removing the pressure, she is actually far more likely to drop me a text at lunchtime saying she is thinking about me! Removing the shame and pressure has allowed her to be herself and communicate when she wants to.

SUPPORTING AN ADHDer STRUGGLING WITH OBJECT CONSTANCY

Relationships are two-way streets. If one person finds daily communication easy and one doesn't, then you're pulling in different directions. The trick is not to see either as right or wrong, but to see both as valid.

Your ADHDer will likely have had a lifetime of masking their difficulties with communication, whereby their best efforts have still led to the collapse of relationships. We don't want them to get better at texting; we want them to feel empowered to be honest about their needs, and in turn, we want to be able to be honest about ours.

BE HONEST: It's important to let your ADHDer know that it can make you feel like they don't care about you if you don't hear from them, that your needs matter too. It's important for you to hear that they really do love you, and for you to understand that digital communication is an area they are struggling with.

REMOVE THE PRESSURE: Let your ADHDer know that you don't expect to hear from them when they are busy with something else, and that it's absolutely okay for them not to message you. And of course if they do, it's welcome! Be clear that if you call or text with something urgent, you do expect them to be there for you. But assure them that daily chitchat is not something they need to engage in to be loved. Give them the freedom to be where they are.

PLAN TOGETHER: If frequent text communication isn't going to be a way you show love for each other, then what is? Figure out ways to spend quality time together face-to-face, where you can really experience the love you have for each other. ADHDers are such incredible company; planning fun and exciting things to do together is a great way to stay connected.

YOU CAN ALWAYS CALL: There are times when I've needed an answer on something fairly urgently from Rox. At those times I'll call her, and if she doesn't answer I'll send a message saying, "I just need to know XYZ. Give me a call when you can." She will always come back to me as soon as possible.

SYMPTOM NINE:
DIRECTIONAL DYSLEXIA

AKA "So sorry… Can you just tell me the way again? Slowly?"
Written by Rox

We've lived in our current house for almost three years.

I still regularly leave and walk the *wrong* way to our local shop.

A journey I have literally done hundreds of times…

Welcome to directional dyslexia.

In my world, verbal directions come in gibberish, Google Maps is a twisted liar, and trains are always going the wrong way. But… if you asked me the location of the childhood den I once built at summer camp, I could walk you there blindfolded. It's like certain places are etched into my brain with a clarity that military forces would be happy with. And everything else? It's a jumble of lefts, rights, wrong turns, new places, and overwhelm. Trying to find a given destination usually leaves me crying on a pavement, or asking the third person in a row for the same directions.

I get lost all the time, obviously. And it can be a pretty traumatic experience.

For example, a few years ago I got a text from a friend. He'd been at a New Year's Eve party that had gotten out of hand. So out of hand, in fact, that he had ended up with a very deep cut in his thumb, and hospital staff were talking to him about amputation. He was a beautiful piano player, so the thought of this was horrendous beyond words for him.

Due to my newfound sobriety, and the least rock 'n' roll New Year's of all time (involving watching a fireplace video on Netflix and being in bed before 10 p.m.), I was awake early on New Year's Day, and able to travel down to London to see him in hospital.

He sent me the address and off I went.

I managed to get the train to London with no problems. I had done that many times before, and it was very familiar, but as I boarded the bus from the train station to take me to the hospital, as advised by Google Maps, anxiety started to set in.

The second I am off-piste, or somewhere I haven't been before, I am utterly overwhelmed by a sense of being lost and hopeless. There's too much to take in. And so the worries begin.

What if I get off on the wrong stop?

What if I can't find his room?

What if he's moved by the time I get there?

What about visiting hours?

Thankfully, between Google Maps and the bus stop names, I was able to make it to the hospital. But the energy it had taken to get there had drained me; my anxiety was high, and I was starting to sweat. And now I was faced with a bigger task: find my friend in this absolute maze of a hospital.

To my absolute dismay, I couldn't even locate the reception.

I found myself walking around the back of the hospital, my hands shaking as I stared at my phone, trying to walk myself closer to where he was. Somehow, with every turn I took, I was further away from him.

Eventually I found a way in… But the sign read *Oncology*. This wasn't right. Walking as fast as I could, I looked for more signs. All of them featured long medical names that I did not recognise. Not one of them said reception, or what I really needed to read: *Your friend is this way*—with a MASSIVE arrow.

I was walking around the hospital for 30 minutes before the overwhelm took over. I felt the familiar sense of hopelessness and a racing heartbeat, as sweat began to pour down my face. Finally, I started weeping as I wandered the hospital corridors. A janitor stopped to ask if I was okay.

I felt absolutely ridiculous, standing there crying in a place where so many people were struggling.

Where so many people were dying.

In Oncology, where family members were saying their last goodbyes.

And there I was, falling apart, because I can't read a map.

The janitor pointed me towards reception, and a few minutes later, I was back on track. I took some deep breaths to calm myself, because I needed to be there for my friend. In the end, he didn't have his thumb amputated. And to this day he still talks about what it meant to him that I was there. He never knew that getting there was so difficult for me.

If I know where I'm going, if I've done the route before, I'm good. For example, getting to London from our current house in Sevenoaks is a piece of cake for me: I know the route off by heart. I can visualise it in full-colour HD, I know the times of the trains, which side of the platform to stand on, and which exit to use at London Bridge if I want to get a coffee before heading into work.

Routine and repetition are my best friends. But the minute I'm going somewhere new? All bets are off. It's like I'm looking at a different world than other people, who seem to navigate new places with the ease that I experience only when I'm moving around somewhere that I know by heart.

I don't see the signs, I miss the door numbers, and very frequently this ends with me crying in the street.

Enter Rich, Mr. Human Satnav. He drives somewhere once and knows the way. He hears a long set of directions and can remember them, and he NEVER walks the wrong way to Tesco out of our house. The fact that we have polar-opposite ways of moving through this world only highlights how much of an issue directions are for me.

Getting my ADHD diagnosis, and learning about directional dyslexia, didn't mean I would suddenly learn to go the right way when I was out and about. But what it did do was remove the shame. Consistently getting lost, not being able to read a map, always being late and crying on the street... The only explanation I had for these behaviours was that I was an absolute idiot. Stupid. Worthless. When your inner narrative is screaming this kind of thing at you on the daily, it ramps up the stress you are already feeling, which of course makes you even worse with directions!

In this case, diagnosis means that I do not have to suffer alone. That I have language to describe what is happening. Now, when I get off the train at the wrong stop, or go the wrong way on the tube, or can't find a building, I will call Rich. He will calm me down, remind me to breathe, and then use his superhuman (AKA neurotypical) directional skills to help me get back on track.

My issues are met with absolute love, acceptance and support. Which means I ask for help so much more than I ever used to. Slowly, the veil of shame has lifted… and guess what? I'm a bit better at getting where I need to be. I'll still walk out of our house and go the wrong way to Tesco, and we'll both laugh and course correct. No shame needed.

SUGGESTIONS TO HELP

Don't leave the house. Ever. Problem solved. Oh, I wish it could be that simple! But we often have to go places that we don't know, and truth is, we're likely going to get lost and overwhelmed. Accepting that rather than fighting it allows us to have a chance of making travel a little easier.

When I say "accept how you work," I don't mean saying, "Oh, I am so terrible with directions because I have ADHD." I do not mean you should accept your moral failing as proof you're an inferior human and get on with it. I mean you need to accept yourself radically, and with love. This means saying, "I struggle with new places and get super-overwhelmed! It's a symptom of my ADHD, and I might need some extra support and kindness."

VISUAL DIRECTIONS: Google Maps, or even well-explained verbal directions from a stranger, just don't cut it. What really helps are visual cues. Get someone to give you landmarks, names of pubs, colours of buildings, and if possible, a photograph of what you are aiming for. The second you can see your destination, somehow the anxiety lifts: it's just so much easier to process and understand.

CALM DOWN IF YOU GET CONFUSED: If you're lost and feel the ADHD overwhelm kicking in (it feels something like a panic attack to me), then take a break. You won't find anything when you're on the verge of tears. Find a bench, have a sit-down, and breathe deeply until you can feel yourself returning to a calmer state. Everything in you will want to rush onward to find where you are going, to try and reduce how late you are going to be, but don't do it: I promise, a good cry and a few deep breaths will have you navigating like a pro.

PLAN JOURNEYS: Planning the night before really helps you visualise your journey and reduce anxiety. For example, know the final destination of your train so you know what to look for on the board. Know whether it's the East or West line of the tube. Know whether it's the main hospital building, or a different entrance. The more information you can gather and write in your notes app before you leave, the better prepared you'll be, and the less chance of a breakdown.

ASK FOR HELP: If you're going to a meeting, to a job interview, or to meet a friend, and you're struggling to find them, give them a ring. It's absolutely okay to ask for landmark directions and let people know you are struggling. Asking for help means you don't have to feel so alone, and often one simple direction later you will be back on the right track. And here's a cool thing: so many times recently when I've asked for help, the person has said, "Oh yeah, it can be really tough to find," which is always a shock to me. Maybe I'm not really stupid after all…

"You're walking the wrong way. Again!"
Written by Rich

"Babe, I'm lost."

I can hear Rox is on the verge of tears.

"I've walked around the outside of the building twice. There is no number 447. I don't know what to do."

Rox and I were going to a joint health check appointment in London. We were travelling separately, as we had both come from work.

I Google Mapped it, and got there with no problems. Rox, it seemed, hadn't been so lucky. Over the phone, I told her to take some deep breaths and reminded her that everything would be okay. I then guided her to where I was, using visual landmarks: the building with the bright red door, the pub with the horse outside the front. Unmissable.

Five minutes later she arrived, flustered and incredibly apologetic that she was late.

She had actually passed the door we were meant to meet at twice—it turns out that the number was hidden, tucked away on a buzzer. Visitors had to walk up the steps to the building and know the clinic name in order to find the right place. (Really not easy, even to a neurotypical!)

Rox knew only the door number, so she had been walking around looking for a large 447 painted on a door—which, unfortunately, didn't exist. Being unable to find the door had overwhelmed her system to the point she couldn't think and was struggling to breathe.

I would challenge anyone in that state to be able to navigate to their destination.

Since her diagnosis, this is something we talk about a lot more, and our discussions are always open, honest, and shame free. Her struggles with directions don't make her stupid, or weird: it's just how her brain works. If we are going somewhere together, I'll handle all the directional stuff, and if she is travelling alone we will always talk about it beforehand. We make sure she has planned the route, left enough time and booked anything she can in advance. It's the little things to reduce stress that really help.

SUPPORTING AN ADHDer WITH DIRECTIONAL DYSLEXIA

So much of our advice has been centred on accepting your ADHDer exactly as they are, allowing a safe space for them to communicate their internal experiences and totally unmask. However, with something like directional dyslexia, there is a real-world need to help them in practical ways.

In this case, acceptance doesn't mean saying that being late and missing flights is okay. That will only make their life more stressful and cause problems at work, or in their personal life. Acceptance means that they are absolutely lovable despite their struggles *and* that you can help and encourage them to find ways to support how they travel.

DON'T JUDGE: It's easy to think someone is being stupid when they can't find something that you find so easily, but that is just not the case. Your ADHDer simply processes new environments very differently, and can easily become overwhelmed. Be a safe space for directional help so they always know they can call you if they're lost and need a friendly voice.

HELP WITH PLANNING: Planning their travel the night before is not something that will come naturally to your ADHDer, so a kind reminder, or even an offer to help, can really change the game for the following day.

DOUBLE-CHECK TRAVEL TIMES: Time blindness can play a big role in getting travel plans wrong for your ADHDer. They will look at the tube journey time, but won't add time to walk on either side of that. They will guesstimate how long it takes to get somewhere in a car without any thought for rush hour. Checking through their travel plan means you can point out any areas where they have underestimated how long things will take, and help them to leave earlier. Don't forget to build in time for getting lost, too: if they have left in good time and still get lost, they won't have the added fear of being late, which makes overwhelm worse.

HELP THEM CALM DOWN: If your ADHDer contacts you while overwhelmed and lost, the first thing to do is to calm them down. Let them know it's going to be okay, and encourage some deep breaths. As soon as they are more regulated, you can then move on to help them with the actual directions.

SYMPTOM TEN: IMPULSIVITY

AKA "We need to buy all of the equipment to make resin, NOW!"

www.house-of-resin.com

www.laterecords.com

www.girlguys.com

Here's a small sample of the domain names I own, covering various business ideas I've had over the years. I'm a passionate collector of 123-reg domains. It's a hobby.

When a business idea forms in my head, it forms fully. I see the logo, the brand name and identity, the first social media posts, and the incredible impact it will have on the world. My brain simply does not see any barriers to entry, like skill or cost. All I see is a beautiful, shiny new business, and myself hurtling towards it at lightning speed, ready to dedicate the rest of my life to it.

I'll open the notes app on my phone and scrawl a few ideas, convinced this one is THE one. Yes, I remind myself, I've been here before. Yes, I have numerous domains and social media accounts lying dormant, but the past does not define the future. Everything has happened before, has happened for *this* idea.

This idea can be anything. Resin making. A record label. A gender-neutral clothing line. Whatever it is, though, it is a matter of urgency that I pursue it vigorously the moment the first thought enters my mind. I simply *must* purchase the domain name, register the social media accounts, look into trademarking and buy all the equipment needed for my new venture.

For anyone interested in how any of these turned out, well, feel free to type the domains into your browser...

One business venture in particular deserves an honourable mention. Rich and I had been dating for three months and were out walking in the local park. That morning, I'd seen someone making a wooden table with a blue resin waterfall running through it. The idea had gripped me hard.

I began dreaming about learning to make one of these resin tables and very quickly decided that this was my new purpose in life. The excitement was flooding through every pore of my being and I had to share it with Rich.

"Babe," I told him, "we should really think about starting a resin business. It's the next big thing."

Rich, of course, had a lot of questions about materials, skills, and cost projections. But my blind optimism and passion won him over. He had no idea that this was a regular occurrence for me, and the poor bloke probably thought he was witnessing the birth of a highly successful e-commerce business.

It wasn't long before we had brainstormed company names, and I was logging on to 123-reg.com to buy the domain name "House of Resin." Over the coming weeks, Rich and I purchased everything we would need to make resin. We watched hours of YouTube tutorials and began to make our first items. The sheer joy that flooded through me when I held that first opal glitter ashtray in my hands was like nothing else I'd ever experienced.

Resin making bought me about three weeks of joy before my enthusiasm started to wane and I realised that my full-time job as a songwriter kind of got in the way, and that resin making was actually pretty hard to do really well. Soon the supplies were moved into a cupboard, where they have remained to this day. I call it the hobbies graveyard.

The timeline from "life purpose" to "I can't be bothered any more" is anywhere from a day to a few months. No matter how many times I do the same thing, no matter all of the evidence to the contrary, I simply HAVE to start a business—the desire to do so is incredibly intense for my ADHD brain. You see, impulsivity is a symptom. In my youth, this meant changing partners, moving countries, and quitting jobs. As I've got older, it's meant starting businesses.

My life has been full of segues that have led me down a series of twinkling, fairy-lit garden paths, only to have me end up bored again—and about £500 worse off.

However… our TikTok account was started in the exact same way, on a random impulse, as you read in the introduction, and that hobby-turned-obsession has led us to connecting with hundreds of thousands of people worldwide. That random impulse has helped us build a community where people learn to understand and reduce the shame of ADHD.

That crazy idea led us to this point—writing the book that you have in your hands. So, although sometimes a business idea for an ADHDer is going to lead nowhere (except the hobbies graveyard), on rare occasions that blind optimism and creativity can lead us somewhere absolutely phenomenal. You see, we ADHDers have this rare ability to fail over and over again and never lose hope. To keep believing the next one is going to work. When people have that kind of persistence, well, the chances of something working eventually are pretty goddamn high.

FAIL

FAIL

FAIL

FAIL

FAIL

FAIL

FAIL

SUCCEED

That's pretty much always what it looks like. So here's to the ADHDers who start their soap-making businesses, who start selling crafts on Etsy, who start writing a book or offering parenting classes, who go into acting, or who open a gluten-free bakery. Here's to the ones who never give up, even though all the data points tell them they are a failure.

Here's to the ones who change the world.

SUGGESTIONS TO HELP

Impulsivity can be a life-changing trait—for the better, and for the worse. On its best days, it's the start of a new business idea that can change the world. On its worst, it's breaking up with someone and moving to a new country only to be filled with regret.

We need to find a way for our impulsivity to work *for* us, as opposed to against us. The starting place for that is accepting that we are very impulsive. We can then balance our ideas with a good dose of logical thinking to find out which ones are worth pursuing!

HAVE PATIENCE: Just because the soap-making venture feels like your purpose today doesn't mean it will tomorrow. Take a beat, and really think about what it involves. Don't just fantasise about the end goal. Is this idea something you are willing to dedicate the next 10 years of your life to? Or is it possible that you have been hit with the intense emotions of a new hobby and dream life but that, in reality, the day-to-day of this job doesn't align with who you are?

FIND YOUR GENIUS: Is there something you were really good at when you were younger? For example, did you excel at acting, music, painting, or science? Often the key to our genius will be embedded in the thing that we naturally gravitated towards. Is it worth going all-in there? If you haven't found your thing yet, don't be discouraged. Allow your imagination to soar; allow yourself to try out different jobs and to experiment with different businesses. The one that connects, that helps others, that adds value, might just be your own forever fixation.

DREAM, DON'T DO: Even if you've already found your forever fixation, I promise you other jobs and business ideas are still going to come, and they can be a dangerous distraction. Allow yourself to dream about a custom-colour hair dye company; come up with the name, even draw yourself a logo. Get all your dopamine out of the idea using your incredible imagination, but don't quit on your forever thing. Don't play against yourself. We need boundaries around creativity to allow us to actually reach the potential we have inside.

FIND YOUR TEAM: Whatever venture you have set out upon, there is value in having a neurotypical person working with you. You each bring different skills to the table. Left brain, right brain, if you will. Where you may lead in creative disruption and blind optimism, they can lead in logic, organisation, and planning. In our case, without Rich, ADHD_Love would have been a five-video TikTok and then I would have got bored. Our success relies equally upon my creativity and his consistency.

"Shall I put the resin stuff in the hobbies graveyard?"
Written by Rich

When our account first started to go viral on TikTok, both Rox and I were incredibly excited. We couldn't wait to get back from work each day to create content on this account together. Coming up with ideas, filming them, getting them online, and then refreshing the app like mad to see if what we had created was connecting with people—it was a joint hobby that brought us so much joy!

A couple of weeks, and a few million video views later, I started to notice the spark had gone for Rox. Something had changed. That childlike mega-enthusiasm had been replaced with a sense of duty, and what almost looked like boredom.

I asked her if she had lost her love for TikTok, and told her that if she had it would be no problem at all. She has a great job as a songwriter, and I have worked for a bank for 20 years. To me, the TikTok venture was a really fun thing for us to do, and we were so grateful for the love we received, but there was never any pressure to continue with it if we weren't both enjoying it.

She explained to me, as only someone with an ADHD diagnosis can, that she falls intensely for new hobbies, that the impulsivity overtakes her and she commits herself fully to this being her new life purpose. Her pattern in the past was quitting when that crazy fire went out. This time, she was committed to carrying on. She could see we were making a tangible difference in people's lives, and she had me to support her.

Over the coming months, we found our mojo: one day we might have three ideas, get them all filmed and feel like we were the next big thing in the influencer world. That would be followed by 10 days of no ideas and no content. But we both persisted, with a kind of wonky consistency you can expect from an ADHD and neurotypical partnership.

Since starting our social media accounts, Rox has had many other ideas, ranging from a fan-funded record label, to a gender-neutral swimwear collection for kids, to a book about ADHD. I'm always amazed by the sheer excitement and brilliance of this type of creativity. What I know is I cannot control or stop the creative genius of Rox's brain: the impulsivity is not something she can turn off. It's how she works. There are no brakes—that's what I'm here for. Our strategy is to let Rox fantasise about her new idea, and I'll get involved in talking it all out, but we will then calmly and rationally decide which ideas we should actually be committing our time to.

If you are currently reading this book, you'll know how that worked out.

SUPPORTING AN ADHDer WITH IMPULSIVITY

Impulsivity has negative connotations. It can sound like a person is doing something wrong, or is careless. And yes, sometimes that may be the case. But wild, creative ideas can be impulsive; the desire to travel or try a new restaurant can be impulsive. Beautiful things can come from impulsivity, too. It's not something to be squashed or judged.

The impulsivity of your ADHDer is something to protect. You can help them to see when an idea might land them in trouble, or, conversely, when an idea might just be that stroke of genius they have waited their whole life for.

DON'T DISMISS DREAMS: When your ADHDer suddenly drops a brand-new life purpose on you, it can feel like the most nonsensical thing you've ever heard. But don't dismiss it. For them, flexing this creative muscle and fantasising about the future is how they experience a lot of happiness. Chat about the ideas, and have some fun yourself—in my case, that meant adding to the business plan of the resin company. In the meantime, you can also calmly be reflecting to them what following this dream would entail and advising patience before leaving a current job or buying yet another domain name.

WATCH AND WAIT: When your ADHDer has a new purpose, they will convince you and anyone who will listen that this thing is 100 percent going to happen. Their intoxicating communication style makes it all the more likely they will be believed. My advice is to watch and wait. This might be a flash in the pan that they will have forgotten about in two weeks (like the time Rox said she was going to train to swim the English Channel), or it might be an incredibly creative idea that could be life-changing. Like when she rolled over one night and said we had to start a couples' TikTok.

PROVIDE A REALITY CHECK: Your ADHDer will have the company name, marketing plan and TED Talk down. But what they probably haven't thought about are the financial implications or practicalities of their grand plans. It can be very helpful to remind them of things like start-up costs and staff budgets, taxes and expansion costs. These are the unsexy details that can help bring them back down to earth. If an ADHDer is willing to get into the unsexy stuff, this might be a sign of staying power.

SPOT THE GOLD: Albert Einstein, Richard Branson, Will Smith, Zooey Deschanel, Walt Disney and Simone Biles are all notable people with ADHD. These are people who can and do (or did) change the world. Ninety-nine of your ADHDer's ideas might go down the drain, but keep your mind open for that one idea that will go to the clouds.

ADHD AND LOVE

Written by Rox

We couldn't write a book about ADHD and *not* talk about how it relates to love. ADHD symptoms don't just affect our ability to do the cleaning or arrive somewhere on time. They can also affect our ability to love somebody deeply, and to receive love in return.

You see, behaviours like impulsivity, dopamine seeking, and getting bored quickly can have a catastrophic effect on your intimate relationships. I genuinely believed I was broken beyond repair in this area. For me, the most damaging side effect of my undiagnosed ADHD was the havoc it caused in my intimate relationships. It stopped me from ever progressing to true intimacy, because I was constantly seeking the new high of somebody else.

There are two reasons why not understanding this connection can have a really negative effect. First, those behaviours can hurt a lot of people. I alienated a lot of good people, who wanted to love me, when my impulsivity dragged me on to somebody new. Second, it's only within a truly safe and secure relationship that we can begin to heal from some of the trauma we have experienced. So, by following my every romantic obsession, I was denying myself a chance to really be known and accepted for who I was at my core. It's when we truly allow ourselves to be seen that we can start slowly to love the parts of us we feel most ashamed of.

Without Rich, I don't know if I could function. This is a little embarrassing to admit, and I imagine many people would label me co-dependent for such a statement. Whatever the judgement on it, though, it's true. I need help to live a stable and happy life. I hope that by sharing the absolute disaster that was my romantic life, I can bring a little hope to those of you who are yet to find your person.

I want to remind you that you aren't bad, or broken, or undeserving of beautiful, intimate love. You just work a little differently. And by understanding those differences, you will be able to access the most wonderful place in the whole world: a true home, built on love, trust, humour, and authenticity. Before this gets too Hallmark, though, let's throw it back to a time when I was the queen of relationship chaos.

While my friends were finding their long-term partners, settling down, and having babies, I seemed to be stuck in a pattern:

- Meet somebody new
- Become utterly obsessed
- Decide they were the one (again)
- Merge lives (often involving moving in together early on)
- Believe I am a sex god

Then… reality starts kicking in.

- I start feeling bored
- I realise I am not in fact a sex god
- I feel scared that I'm losing something I thought was stability
- In order to take my mind off how sad all this is, I leave
- Repeat cycle

Each time, when those crazy highs from the beginning began fading, the only narrative I had for that was that I wasn't in love anymore.

If normal people have a honeymoon, ADHD people have a treacle sun. It's sweeter, it's brighter, and goddamn, is it going to burn you.

I have had ten serious long-term relationships, all lasting about a year. I've been with men older than me, younger than me, and women. Every time, I'd bring them home to meet my dad and tell him the same thing:

"It's different this time. They're amazing. Just wait until you meet him / her."

Of course it wasn't different, though. It was exactly the same.

In 2018, I got sober from alcohol. I also decided that I was going to get sober from love, from the effect it had on me—the obsessions, the cravings, the secrecy. For me love was a drug. So, I put myself on the bench from dating and committed to 18 months of celibacy. During this time I started a therapy journey that would lead me to an ADHD diagnosis.

Then I met Rich. I was sober, the healthiest I'd ever been mentally and physically, and this time I could say with absolute confidence, "This time it's different." Not because Rich was different, not because I had finally found that magical person, but because *I* was different. I had done the hard work of understanding myself and my patterns, so I knew what to look out for.

The treacle sun, of course, still hit me like a truck, and the intense feelings I had for Rich could only be described as falling in love from the top of a 20-story building. And of course, after six months of absolute romantic bliss, those crazy highs started to disappear. And oh my god, was I petrified. My mind began racing.

Is it happening again?

Am I falling out of love?

But I've done everything right…?

Here is the difference. Rather than run off, fall in lust with somebody else and leave this relationship, I chose to dig in, to face uncomfortable truths and excruciating vulnerability. Looking into the eyes of somebody you love deeply and saying "I'm so scared that my feelings are changing" is one of the most terrifying things I've ever done.

With the honesty and communication that comes with a mid-30s relationship when both people have done therapy, we were able to make it through. I watched him cry at the thought that it might be over, and he held me in his arms on nights when I was incredibly confused and dissociating out of any feelings at all.

That period lasted a few weeks, and we made it through. Where my historical pattern was to cut and run, choosing to stay and dig deeper was like unlocking the secret door hidden in the new love room that gets you into the *real* love room.

This is where the best stuff is: on the other side of the treacle sun. Nobody gets burned here, and there are no crazy highs; there's something so much better. Long-term, beautiful, safe, honest partnership. I was in love, for the first time in my entire life.

How's that for "different this time"?

After getting my ADHD diagnosis, and doing the fresh-ADHDer hyperfocus on every book, podcast and TikTok I could consume on the subject, I heard people I considered heroes talking about what I had struggled so hard with. Finally, I had language for something that had been a lifelong struggle and source of shame for me:

People can be a hyperfocus.

Wait... what?!

PEOPLE CAN BE A HYPERFOCUS.

Hold on... So I am not an evil homewrecker sent from the gates of hell, hexed to walk this earth causing heartbreak wherever I go? I just have ADHD and fall in love very hard because of it? Well, that's enlightening...

Makes sense, though, right?

If I can fall in love with resin making and dedicate my life to it overnight, no wonder I'm falling in love left, right and centre with every person who crosses my path.

Armed with this knowledge, I had a choice when faced with a new love interest: maybe this wasn't love I was feeling. Maybe it was just an intense crush, intensified by my ADHD. I now realise I don't need to run away with someone just because I have a little crush, any more than I need to quit my current job for my resin empire.

What I do need to do, though, is get really honest with myself and my partner about how I work. Those first conversations I had with Rich, where I shared how easily I get attracted to people and how intense those attractions can be, were excruciating. But he leaned in with curiosity, and I got more and more comfortable with being honest.

Rich and I now laugh about the way my brain works. He will often check in with me and ask, "Any hyperfocuses going on at work?"

In simple terms, "Have you got feelings for anybody else?" If I did, I know we would talk about it and make a plan together. Love is an incredibly complicated topic for everyone. But for ADHDers, it can be the most shameful part of our lives. If you are living in fantasy land, not present with your partner, always destroying great relationships for something new, then I hope this chapter helps you find peace, stability and the home that you really deserve.

There is no shame in feeling attractions to others. We cannot help the way we feel. What we *can* help, though, is how we act on those feelings. Rather than keep secrets, which leads to pain for everyone involved, we are called to the harder task of sharing our most intimate selves with somebody else and allowing ourselves to be completely known.

SUGGESTIONS TO HELP

Honestly, for so many neurodivergents, life is about masking. About covering up that which we find so shameful, even in intimate relationships. The problem is, that leaves us unknown for our whole lives. And it's in the very act of being utterly known, in all our glory and failure, that we find true happiness and healing. When we feel loved, despite all the things we see as flaws? Well, that's where the real healing happens.

Getting there doesn't come easily for everybody, and staying there is a lot of hard work. Relationship dynamics are extremely complex, affected by our histories, different brains, attachments, and the relationships we had and witnessed with our caregivers. If you spot a pattern that is causing you or others pain, please consider that you may need a little extra support.

USE YOUR ADHD LENS: If you have a history of leaving, cheating, or self-destructing, and you have ADHD, I want you to stop calling yourself horrendous names and believing you are deeply flawed. Look at your behaviour with compassion, not judgement. I absolutely do not condone cheating, mind you, and ADHD should never be an excuse, but once you know that love is a hyperfocus, a dopamine hit, just like an expensive shopping cart or a new hobby, you can begin to take accountability and change.

USE RADICAL HONESTY: We've often learned to hide huge parts of ourselves—our funny dances, our childlike nature, our obsessional minds, and perhaps most of all how hard and how quickly we can fall into a hole and call it love. True love asks a lot of you, and part of that is radical honesty. It means telling your partner if you feel disconnected, if you've got an attraction to someone else. Handle this with the utmost care, though, because those things are not easy to hear. In an emotionally healthy mature relationship, however, you and your partner will be able to handle it. Learn to see the way you love as a problem to be solved together, not as something to fight with alone.

BE ACCOUNTABLE: ADHDers are impulsive by nature—think of the shopping cart that gets overfilled and put on the credit card that we have just paid off. The mullet haircut we get after spending four years growing out our hair. The drink we say yes to with the person we know could burn us. We have to take accountability and set up boundaries so that those we love can feel safe. You can't be impulsive with lust. You will hurt everyone. If you are in a relationship and that fantasy starts to happen with somebody else—that dopamine rush hitting you like a class A drug—step away, and stay sober. It doesn't come easy, but my god, nothing worth having ever does.

GET THERAPY: ADHD played a massive role in the impulsivity of my lust life, but so did other things. A high percentage of people with ADHD will have grown up in a home with at least one parent with emotional difficulties. Those difficulties, which sometimes manifest as ADHD, cause problems for the child around intimacy, vulnerability and communication, three necessities for happy relationships. Therapy, in particular attachment-focused trauma therapy, might be needed to help unlearn negative behaviours.

"Falling in love with anyone else this week, babe?"
Written by Rich

"I don't know what's happened to my feelings."

My heart sank into my stomach, and I felt the blood drain from my face.

Sat in front of me, hunched over, teary-eyed, and very confused, was the person I had fallen in love with. The person I absolutely knew was the one I wanted to spend my life with.

Every instinct in me told me to run away. To pack my bag and leave tonight. I was staring heartbreak right in the face. I'd been there before, and I didn't have it in me to go through it again. I've had two failed marriages in my life, both incredibly traumatic experiences, and the thought of once again undergoing even a shadow of that pain was unbearable.

At the time Rox spoke those words, I was going through therapy myself, to work through some sexual abuse that I had experienced as a child. Thank God I was, because it was in those sessions that I had learned to regulate my own emotions and had learned the ability to respond, not react.

It took everything in me, but I was able to be curious with Rox about what was happening, and even though it hurt like hell, I found empathy for what she was explaining.

We had built our relationship on an extremely strong foundation of trust. And for the first time, rather than running, I was able to sit, and stay, and talk through some of the hardest emotions we can have as human beings.

Those conversations led us to be closer, more intimate, and more in love than we had ever been. It's a love I honestly didn't know was possible.

When Rox was first diagnosed, she came to me crying, and showed me a TikTok: it was a creator explaining why lust and love hit ADHD people so much harder. Seeing it through an ADHD lens not only set her free from the decades of shame over her relationship struggles, but it also helped me. She wasn't falling out of love; she was crashing down to earth from the most intense emotional experience we can ever go through. It's not that she didn't love me, I realised; it's that she was incredibly confused at her changing emotional state, and up until now, had never had the language to explain her experience.

As the years have gone on, what was for us an incredibly hard time has become somewhat of an in-joke. We giggle at her changing emotions, and have really honest chats about whether she is hyperfocusing on anybody else.

Loving someone with ADHD will be the most exhilarating and passionate thing you've ever experienced, and you have to be strong enough to catch them when they crash down. We have a relationship that, due to my own childhood, I never thought I would be able to have. It's joyful, trusting, difficult, honest, hilarious and vulnerable all at the same time, and I am so grateful for the therapy that we have both done and the understanding of ADHD that we both now have. I really hope this chapter can help you navigate difficult times, and find your own key to the secret room of real love.

SUPPORTING AN ADHDer WITH LOVE

The foundation for true love is intimacy. It's being completely known by another person, and being loved. For an ADHDer, so much of who they are has remained hidden from the world—huge chunks of their identity they have considered too shameful to be loved. It's the sharing of these shameful secrets that will allow them to experience true intimacy. Love, as with anything worth having, takes hard work and radical honesty. It means choosing connection over fear, and being on the same team no matter what you face.

CHOOSE CURIOSITY OVER JUDGEMENT: If your ADHDer is telling you the difficulties they are having in the relationship, get curious, not angry. Don't shame them; ask them "What does that feel like for you?" and "How are you doing?" Connecting to someone's struggle will help you empathise and not take it as a personal attack.

SET BOUNDARIES: Your emotions matter too. As much as you need to hold space for your ADHD partner, they need to hold space for you. During times of sadness and confusion, both people in the relationship deserve, soft, safe, curious communication. These are the markers of a healthy relationship.

USE HUMOUR: Your ADHDer's history of relationship problems probably comes with a lot of shame. Using humour can let them know that nothing is shameful in this relationship and that all parts of them are welcome. For example, I'll joke with Rox over a game of Mario Kart: "Just checking you haven't fallen out of love today, babe." Making light of something that has felt so heavy for both of you is a great way to bond.

DO YOUR RESEARCH: Learn about ADHD and relationships, about attachment styles and about healthy communication. There are so many incredible books and podcasts out there that will give you the tools you need to have those hard conversations. Love, like anything worth having, is something you must both work at on a daily basis.

THE JOYS OF ADHD

Written by Rox

Remember my story from earlier in the book about hiding under the bed in my basement flat a few years ago, petrified by the loud sounds of the workmen ripping out and replacing my electricity supply with a pay-as-you-go meter, utterly ashamed and with no idea how I was going to tell my landlord what had happened? (Or stay organised enough to keep the lights on?) In the face of those sorts of incidents, and some of the other things we've talked about, it's very difficult to think about the *joys* of ADHD.

I want to be really clear: my being able to talk about the joys of ADHD now is coming from a place of real privilege. I was able to spend many months with an incredible trauma therapist who fundamentally changed how I viewed myself. Add to that my own personal choices relating to sobriety, and my commitment to a long-term partner, and I'm now in a really stable place. Without Rich, therapy, or sobriety, I wouldn't be able to talk about any benefits of ADHD.

If you are in a place where your world is falling apart, where you feel stuck in life and ashamed, if you're drowning in debt, perhaps self-medicating with drugs or alcohol, then this section may be hard to read. I want you to know that I've been exactly where you are, and it's my hope that you get the support and help that you deserve, so that one day you may come out from under the rock that unsupported ADHD can have you living under.

So much of the discourse around ADHD relates to the more negative symptoms, all of which I have many anecdotes for, many of which have been shared in this book: the chronic forgetfulness, the inability to prioritise, a cavalier attitude with money. These things are enough to destroy somebody's life, just as the shame-reducing knowledge of a diagnosis and support from loved ones and therapists can go a long way toward mending it again.

This book wouldn't be complete without sharing some of the wonderful things ADHD has bought me. Below is a list of just some of the things I am grateful for.

OPTIMISM: I have a relentless mindset of positivity about what can be achieved, often not seeing the problems or hurdles that a neurotypical person might be hindered by. This has allowed me to dedicate my life to music and find success as both a songwriter and an artist in my late 30s.

QUICK LEARNING: In the music industry nowadays, there is an insatiable desire for content. Historically, anyone entering the business would need to pay stylists, videographers and editors; however, ADHD means I can learn a skill that I'm passionate about very quickly. With Pinterest boards and some wonderful apps, I'm able to create lyric and performance videos from the comfort of my own home.

PROBLEM SOLVING: My brain will always find a way through. There's a famous Bill Gates quote that goes, "I choose a lazy person to do a hard job, because a lazy person will find an easy way to do it." I can't help but wonder if Mr. Gates was actually talking about a person with ADHD.

BRAINSTORMING: If you need a business name, I'll have 50 ideas for you within two minutes. When I need titles for new songs and EPs, my notes app is filled with hundreds of ideas. When a brand approaches me and Rich to make an advert for them on our TikTok, I will have a plethora of fun and engaging ways to do this... My brain is essentially always brainstorming!

RISK TAKING: Sometimes in life, you have to take a risk to change your life in a big way. For example, starting our ADHD_Love TikTok led us to writing a book and Rich taking a year off the stable job he has had in a bank for 20 years. My appetite for risk has absolutely been a driving force in the decisions we've made to get to this point.

EMPATHY: I find it incredibly easy to sense what people are feeling and what they need, probably from a lifetime of being misunderstood myself. I'm incredibly passionate about making the people I love feel safe and heard. I am also a stepmum to two incredible kids, and I'm so grateful for the way I am able to feel their unspoken struggles. This has helped bring about a lot of healing in our house.

CREATIVITY: My mind is constantly creating. Working in music as I do, this is such a good fit. I'm constantly inspired by both the real and digital worlds I live in, and I'm able to think of really interesting ways to speak about these things in songs. I'm as happy painting something in a pottery shop as I am doing science experiments with my eight-year-old stepdaughter. If it's creative, I can throw myself into it heart first.

CRISIS SITUATIONS: When something really difficult is happening, I can be really calm, see a clear way through and help move people through what might seem impossible. Again, this is a skill I most likely developed from a lifetime of overcoming things that felt impossible to me.

There are so many other positive things I could speak about, but I don't want to overwhelm you. I truly hope some items on this list resonate with you, and if they don't, I hope they can at least bring a little encouragement to you regarding what may lie ahead in the future. As you come to the end of this book, I want you to know that from the first crazy idea to upload a TikTok, to my hyperfocus on sharing so much of our lives, to the wild idea that we could write a book, every step of the way has been led and inspired by ADHD.

With the right support, a neurodivergent brain can be a world-changing brain. I hope this book helps you get the love you deserve, and that it reminds you of the power you hold to change the world.

The Joys of Loving Someone with ADHD
Written by Rich

Rox's ADHD has been something we've both had to work hard to understand and support. For me, this meant ultimately shifting from my initial mindset of frustration to one of compassion. This, and the hard work Rox has done on her part, has absolutely changed the quality of love we both experience in our house.

As Rox said earlier, people don't speak enough about the incredible things that come along with ADHD. So now I want to take this opportunity to talk about some of the wonderful benefits Rox's ADHD has brought me.

VERY CARING: From the moment I met Rox, she cared deeply about me and my two kids, encouraging me and supporting me through therapy that has fundamentally changed and healed my relationship with my children. Rox is the first to notice when something is wrong with any of us and will make a point to make space for us to talk about it and move through it.

SENSE OF HUMOUR: If I had to choose the most common sound that rings through our house, it would be laughter. Whether she's funny dancing as she cleans her teeth, tripping down the stairs or retelling some elaborate story, she always has me in stitches. There is so much joy around her, it's hard for others not to feel it too.

ENTREPRENURIALISM: It was Rox's vision and belief that not only got us making videos, but also helped us decide we needed to write a book to speak more directly to the community we were building. Coupled with my practicality and organisation, we are a bit of a dream team. She is able to envision a better world and how to get there, and I'm able to support us on the way.

INTERESTS: Last year I found myself on a four-day trip to the Scottish highlands with Rox. It was fascinating learning about Scottish history and in particular the battle of Culloden. Rox and I had watched every season of *Outlander*, which resulted in her hyperfocusing on learning more about Scottish history. So much of what I have learned and experienced is due to her thirst for knowledge.

RESEARCH: From our first family holiday to the Cotswolds, where Rox created and printed out a seven-page itinerary for me and the kids, to the fact that we are members of an off-the-beaten-track spa near our house that I didn't even know existed, to the number of incredible unknown restaurants we have experienced, the level of research Rox puts into every aspect of living makes me feel like we are always uncovering a secret. Life next to her is extremely exciting and fulfilling.

A Few Final Words…

As this book draws to a close, I want to thank the community we have met through the digital world for making us both feel much more understood. It's your comments—which sometimes have us hysterically laughing, or crying, or both, because we relate so much—that have given us the courage to share more of our lives in this book.

If you are lucky enough to love someone with ADHD, it's our hope that this book helps you to understand them and see through a lens of compassion, which will ultimately help them to flourish as the incredible human being they are. I hope you all find the love and support in your current or future relationships that Rox and I have found in each other.

ADHD DICTIONARY

**Disclaimer: These *might* not appear in the official Oxford English Dictionary...

CONVERCOASTER: jumping topics mid-conversation, much like a rollercoaster

CRAFTERNOON: avoiding what you're meant to be doing with a new arts and crafts hobby

DOOM PILES: when you are meant to be tidying up, but you just end up leaving piles all over the house

DOPAMINING: mining for dopamine, usually in the form of overspending on the internet or researching your new favourite hobby

DRAWERGANISE: organising drawers in a manic fashion; at least one of these usually ends up being just a junk drawer

DULLEMMA: when you have two important but uninteresting tasks to do, so you do neither

FLIEVE MINUTES: when you say you only need five minutes, but that is in fact a lie

FLOORDROBE: a floor space, usually carpet, that is also used as a wardrobe

HIDY UP: when you decide to hide things in bags, or under the bed, instead of actually tidying up

INTERHEAD: when you feel like you have 100 internet browser tabs open in your brain at once

INTERNEST: when you have done far too much people-ing and need to lie down in a fort made of pillows and doom scroll

MOOVERING: when you are meant to be cleaning, specifically Hoovering, but you just end up moving things around the house

NOTIVATION: the inability to either begin or complete a low-dopamine task

NOWEVER: when something is getting done either right now or literally never, and you don't know yet which one it is

PROCRASTIWORKING: working really hard on a task, just not the one you're meant to be working on

SIDE QUEST: when you are meant to be doing something, and go off and start doing something else without telling anybody

SNACCIDENT: when you go to the cupboard for a small snack, and end up bingeing on everything in sight

TEXPECTATION: when other human beings text you and expect an instant reply, not knowing that your brain doesn't work like that